ISLAMOPHOBIA AND ANTI-AMERICANISM

CAUSES AND REMEDIES

ISLAMOPHOBIA AND ANTI-AMERICANISM

CAUSES AND REMEDIES

EDITED BY MOHAMED NIMER

amana publications

First Edition 1428AH/2007AC
Printed in the United States of America by International Graphics

Library of Congress Cataloging-in-Publication Data

Islamophobia and anti-Americanism : causes and remedies /
edited by Mohamed Nimer.
        p. cm.
  Includes bibliographical references.
  ISBN 978-1-59008-045-0
 1. Islam--Public opinion. 2. Public opinion--United States.
3. United States--Foreign public opinion. 4. Public opinion
--Islamic countries. 5. Islamic
countries--Relations--United States. 6. United
States--Relations--Islamic countries. I. Nimer, Mohamed, 1960-

  HN90.P8.I85 2007
  305.6'970973--dc22
  2007019328

CONTENTS

CONTRIBUTORS

ASMA AFSARUDDIN

Dr. Asma Afsaruddin is an associate professor of Arabic and Islamic studies at the University of Notre Dame (Notre Dame, IN). Her fields of research are Islamic political and religious thought, the Qur'an and Hadith, Islamic intellectual history, and gender issues. She is the author and editor of three books, the most recent being *Excellence and Precedence: Medieval Islamic Discourse on Legitimate Leadership* (Leiden: 2002). Afsaruddin has served as the chair of the Center for the Study of Islam and Democracy (CDIS) board of directors and is an advisor for Karamah, a women's and human rights organization. She was recently named a Carnegie Scholar for 2005 by the Carnegie Corporation.

PARVEZ AHMED

Dr. Parvez Ahmed is the Chairman of the Board for the Council on American-Islamic Relations (CAIR). He is an Associate Professor of Finance at the University of North Florida in Jacksonville. In addition to his active academic life, he writes editorials dispelling stereotypes about Islam and Muslims. His articles have been published in several leading newspapers around the country. Dr. Ahmed also serves as an at-large board member for the American Civil Liberties Union (ACLU) in Florida. He is also a board member for OneJax, formerly the National Conference on Community and Justice (NCCJ).

SCOTT ALEXANDER

Scott Alexander is associate professor of Islam and director of Catholic-Muslim Studies at the Catholic Theological Union (Chicago, IL). He holds a Ph.D. in the history of religions, with a concentration in Islamic studies from Columbia University and is editor of *Sisters: Women, Religion, and Leadership in Christianity and Islam.* Alexander has led numerous interfaith dialogues in order to bring Muslims, Jews, and Christians in Chicago to a discourse on commonalities.

JAMAL BADAWI

Jamal Badawi is a professor in the Departments of Religious Studies and Management at Saint Mary's University (Halifax, NS, Canada). He completed his undergraduate studies in Cairo, Egypt, and earned his M.A. and Ph.D. at Indiana University (Bloomington, IN) in Business Administration. Dr. Badawi is a highly sought after lecturer in North America and abroad. He is the producer of a 352-segment television series on Islam, *Islam in Focus*, shown on many local television stations in Canada, the United States, and other countries. He also wrote *Gender Equity in Islam: Basic Principles* (American Trust Publications: 1995) and *Leadership: An Islamic Perspective* (Amana Publications: 1999).

CHERIF BASSIOUNI

Dr. M. Cherif Bassiouni is a distinguished research professor of law at DePaul University's (Chicago, IL) College of Law and president of its International Human Rights Law Institute. He has served the United Nations as a member and then chairman of the Security Council's Commission to Investigate War Crimes in the Former Yugoslavia (1992-94) and was appointed by the United Nations High Commissioner for Human Rights as its independent expert on human rights in Afghanistan (2004). Professor Bassiouni has written 24 books, edited 44 books, and authored 217 articles on international criminal law, comparative criminal law, international human rights law, and a wide range of other legal issues.

Contributors

LOUIS CANTORI

Dr. Louis J. Cantori received his Ph.D. from the University of Chicago (Chicago, IL) in political science. He studied Islamic philosophy for one year in the Faculty of Theology at al-Azhar University (Cairo, Egypt). He is the author or editor of four books, including *Local Politics and Development in the Middle East* (Westview Press: 1984), as well as the author of over forty articles. A former president of the American Council for the Study of Islamic Societies, he teaches political science at the University of Maryland, Baltimore County (Baltimore, MD) and serves as a distinguished visiting lecturer at the US Department of State.

RICHARD CIZIK

Richard Cizik, vice president of the National Association of Evangelicals' (NAE) governmental affairs office and is the editor of the organization's *Washington Insight*. He also directs its *Washington Insight* briefing and Christian student leadership conferences, setting its policy direction on issues before Congress, the White House, and the Supreme Court, and serves as a national spokesman on issues of concern to evangelicals.

ANWAR IBRAHIM

Anwar Ibrahim is the former deputy prime minister and finance minister of Malaysia, as well as the founder of the country's Muslim Youth Movement (ABIM). Mr. Ibrahim has experienced political persecution. In 1999, he was sentenced after a highly controversial trial to six years in prison. However, in 2004 an appeals court reversed the second conviction and ordered his release. He now lectures on topics related to Islam and the West at Georgetown University (Washington, DC).

JAMES JONES

James Jones is an associate professor of world religions and African studies at Manhattanville College (Purchase, NY). He is the former chair of the World Religions Department and visiting professor at the Graduate School of Islamic and Social Sciences (Ashburn, VA). His research and lecture activities focus on Muslim American identity and conflict resolution. Jones holds a B.A. in History from Hampton Institute, an M.A. in Religion from Yale University Divinity School, and a D.Min. (Doctorate of Ministry) in Christian-Muslim Relations from Hartford Seminary.

HAFIZ AL-MIRAZI

Hafez al-Mirazi is the Washington Bureau Chief for Al-Jazeera Television. Previously, he was a correspondent for the BBC's Arabic/World Service in Washington, DC, and a talk-show host for the Arab News Network and the Arab Network of America. He also held positions as a writer, editor, and broadcaster for the Voice of America. He holds a B.A. in political science from Cairo University (Cairo, Egypt) and an M.A. in world politics from the Catholic University of America (Washington, DC).

CHIP PITTS

Chip Pitts, president of Bill of Rights Defense Committee and former chairperson of Amnesty International USA's board, is an international attorney, investor/entrepreneur, and law educator who advises businesses. A former chief legal officer of Nokia, Inc. and partner at a major global law firm, he now lectures on law at Stanford University Law School, where he had obtained his law degree. He is a member of the Council on Foreign Relations and the Pacific Council on Foreign Policy.

Contributors

LOUAY SAFI

Dr. Louay Safi is the director of the ISNA Leadership Development Center (ILDC) (Plainfield, IN). He also serves on the board of several leading Muslim organizations and publications, including the Center for the Study of Islam and Democracy (CSID), *Islamic Horizons,* and the Association of Muslim Social Scientists (AMSS). He received a Ph.D. in political science from Wayne State University and is the author of *Peace and the Limits of War* (The International Institute of Islamic Thought: 2001).

CLAUDE SALHANI

Claude Salhani is UPI's international editor with expertise in matters regarding the Middle East, terrorism, and Islam. During his thirty-year career, Salhani has traveled to over seventy-five countries to cover major events. In 1998, he published his memoirs of covering the Middle East in *Black September to Desert Storm: A Journalist in the Middle East* (University of Missouri Press: 1998). During his career, he traveled with and reported on several American presidents as well as foreign dignitaries. He has been based in Beirut, Cairo, Paris, Brussels, London, New York City, and Washington, DC.

SAMER SHAHATA

Samer Shehata teaches Middle East studies at Georgetown University (Washington, DC). During the 2002-2003 academic year, he served as acting director of the Masters of Arts in Arab Studies program. Before coming to Georgetown, he spent one year as a fellow at the Society of Fellows at Columbia University; another year as director of Graduate Studies at New York University's Center for Near Eastern Studies; and taught at the American University in Cairo. In the spring of 2002, he developed a popular course (co-taught with Michael Hudson) on "The US, the Middle East, and the War on Terrorism," which he continues to teach. Shehata holds a Ph.D. in political science from Princeton University.

Muzammil Siddiqi

Dr. Muzammil Siddiqi is the director of the Islamic Society of Orange County (Garden Grove, CA). He served two terms (1997-2001) as president of the Islamic Society of North America. Siddiqi received his early education at Aligarh Muslim University and Darul Uloom Nadwatul Ulama, Lucknow, India. He graduated from the Islamic University of Madinah in 1965 with a higher degree in Arabic and Islamic studies. He received an M.A. in theology from Birmingham University (England) and a Ph.D. in comparative religion from Harvard University. He is a member of the Council of 100 of the World Economic Forum, based in Switzerland.

Shanta Premawardhana

The Reverend Dr. Shanta D. Premawardhana is a Baptist pastor and director of Interfaith Relations, National Council of Churches. For the past fourteen years, he has been the senior pastor of Chicago's Ellis Avenue Church and active in the Hyde Park and Kenwood Interfaith Council. From 1996-98, he served as president of that organization, which currently includes thirty-eight Christian, Hindu, Jewish, and Muslim congregations and organizations. Premawardhana received his seminary education in Sri Lanka and India. He went on to earn an M.A. in comparative religion at Northwestern University and a Ph.D. in the phenomenology of religions.

Contributors

JOHN VOLL

John O. Voll is professor of Islamic history and associate director
of the Prince Alwaleed bin Talal Center for Muslim-Christian
Understanding at Georgetown University (Washington, DC). The
second edition of his book, *Islam: Continuity and Change in the
Modern World* was published by Syracuse University Press in 1994.
He taught Middle Eastern, Islamic, and world history at the
University of New Hampshire for thirty years before moving to
Georgetown in 1995. He graduated from Dartmouth College in
History and received his Ph.D. degree in History and Middle East
studies from Harvard University. He has lived in Cairo, Beirut, and
Sudan and has traveled widely in the Muslim world.

PREFACE

INTEREST in the expressions and ramifications of Islamophobia and anti-Americanism has increased tremendously, especially after the terrorist attacks of September 11, 2001. But the problems subsumed under these two labels have much deeper roots. The concern has become global, with the United Nations taking measures to address anti-American attacks in 2001 and opening forums of discussion about Islamophobia in 2004. On May 13-15, 2005, the Council on American-Islamic Relations (CAIR) held a two-day conference to explore the causes of these two phenomena, both of which are harmful to American Muslims.

In this volume, Dr. Mohamed Nimer assembles university professors, journalists, researchers, community activists, and faith leaders who were asked to define, analyze, and contextualize the forces and events that reinforce anti-American and anti-Muslim feelings. The contributions may open up venues in public discourse that could enable us pinpoint effective remedies. The discussions offer valuable explanations of the problems shaping relations between America and the Muslim world. What emerges from the reflections of experts and leaders is that injustice and extremism are intertwined. Governmental and non-governmental entities have roles to play in the ending of policies and behavior that lead to anger and destruction.

I hope that readers find answers in this collection to many of the pressing questions of our time.

Nihad Awad

Executive Director

Council on American-Islamic Relations

INTRODUCTION: ISLAMOPHOBIA AND ANTI-AMERICANISM ARE MUTUALLY REINFORCING

Mohamed Nimer

T O APPRECIATE THE grave dangers of Islamophobia and anti-Americanism, one must be clear about their essence—what they are and what they are not. A critical study of Islam or Muslims is not Islamophobic. Likewise, a disapproving analysis of American history and government is not anti-American. Contributors to this volume decry the hate directed at a faith community or a people because they happen to be Muslim or American. One can disagree with Islam or with what some Muslims do without having to be hateful. Similarly, one can oppose American policies without hating America as a nation.

These demarcations may sound clear and simple, and yet both Islamophobia and anti-Americanism are on the rise. Anti-Muslim feelings in the United States have intensified, especially after the terrorists attacks of September 11, 2001 (hereafter referred to as 9/11). Between one-fourth and one-third of Americans hold negative views of Islam and Muslims.[1] Opinion leaders, especially on Internet blogs, talk radio, and cable television are increasingly using harsh language to refer to the Islamic faith. Franklin Graham, Jerry Falwell and Pat Robertson, religious leaders often courted by government officials and politicians, have called Islam "a wicked religion", the Prophet Muhammad "a terrorist," and Muslims "worse than Nazis."

A global survey of world public opinion about the United States in November 2005 revealed that uneasy feelings were mutual. In five major Muslim-majority countries, 51 percent to 79 percent of the respondents expressed unfavorable view of the United States. The survey found that sources of dislike were rooted in opposition to American policies in the Muslim world, particularly the war in Iraq and support for Israel.[2]

While such views do not necessarily meet our definition of anti-Americanism, evidence shows that Muslims do hold strong negative stereotypes of westerners in general and Americans in particular. A June 2006 Pew Research Center poll found "pluralities in all of the predominantly Muslim countries surveyed associate Westerners with being greedy, arrogant, immoral, selfish and violent. And solid majorities in Jordan, Turkey and Egypt—as well as a plurality of Muslims in Nigeria—view Westerners as being fanatical."[3]

Beyond agreeing with negative statements about Americans, there is agitation that invokes anti-American feelings. Muslim radicals blame America for most of the Muslim world's problems, even in areas where America is not a player. For example, Bin Laden repeatedly held American imperialism responsible for the persecution of Muslims in the Indian state of Assam.

Bin Laden's faulty rationale goes like this: the exercise of American power has left Muslims unable to support vulnerable Muslim minorities, such as those in India. But there is no link between the rise of American power and the persecution of Muslims in Assam. In fact the general weakness of Muslim-majority countries predated the rise of American power in global affairs.

The reflective papers contained in this publication shed light on the causes and remedies to Islamophobia and anti-Americanism. The questions they attempt to address include: What factors have led to this unfortunate state of affairs? What remedies should be sought to ameliorate prejudice? What is the role of faith leaders in promoting dialogue and tolerance? Can American Muslims bridge the gap of misunderstanding? Most of the following articles suggest that Islamophobia and anti-Americanism are related to one another as well as to politics, policy, the media, and global relations. The contributions draw on American history, religious knowledge, and keen observations of political and historical dynamics.

As suggested clearly throughout this volume, charges of Islamophobia and anti-Americanism are often used as tools in what Louay Safi calls the "war of ideas." John Voll reminds readers that American history is replete with this "old politics"—the practice of dismissing opponents as unpatriotic elements acting outside the national consensus. Voll shows how this resort to politics by intimidation took place since the early days of the American republic. The term *McCarthyism* was coined to describe the anti-communist hysteria in the 1940s and 1950s. According to a renowned legal scholar, David Cole, the targeting of Muslims after 9/11 is a repeat of that history, which included similar draconian executive orders, problematic administrative procedures, constitutionally questionable prosecutions, inquisitive congressional hearings, and fear-driven public discourse—much of which is based on guilt by association.[4]

Of course, this is not to suggest that hateful expressions lack substantive meaning on their own, but to make the case that they should be understood in context. In this connection the following papers emphasize a number of themes, which I attempt to bring into focus in the remainder of this introduction.

REAL GRIEVANCES

Islamophobia and anti-Americanism have been fueled by real grievances. Unjust American policies cause anti-American feelings, while terrorism stirs up Islamophobia. Asma Afsaruddin points out that the American projection of power (whether direct or by proxy, as in the case of Israel) has harmed Muslims in several countries, including Iraq and Afghanistan. Louis Cantori reports on attending a public meeting in 2004, at which returning members of the American occupation administration in Iraq expressed exhilaration regarding what they saw as successful American imperialism.

The United States is looking out for its own interests. But many of the world's Muslims perceive its policies as a leading factor in stifling their progress and denying them genuine political reform. There is no doubt that the American invasion of Iraq has reinforced this perception. The false pretext of weapons of mass destruction used to justify this military endeavor added to the already existing fury in many parts of the Muslim world, where people saw the resulting intervention as a campaign having the broad aim of weakening Muslims.

Chip Pitts expounds on another element of American policies that alienate Muslims, arguing that human rights violations fuel anti-American emotions. Chief among the incidents that inflamed the passions of people around the world were the despicable acts of torture at Iraq's Abu Gharib detention center and other American holding facilities. Other incidents include the legal limbo faced by many Muslims detained by America around the world (including such clearly innocent people as the Canadian citizen Maher Arrar) and who were turned over to other governments to be tortured, and the detention and special registration procedures imposed on thousands of innocent Arab and Muslim immigrants living in America.

Every act of terrorism carried out by extremist Muslims pushes Islmophobes to new extremes. None of the contributors to this volume challenges the truthfulness of this statement. Of course, some may point out that one person's terrorist is another person's freedom fighter. But there is no moral justification whatsoever for attacking civilians. Unfortunately, many Muslims feel helpless when it comes to arresting the scourge of terrorism posed by the likes of al-Qaidah because of the political chaos in the Muslim world, which American foreign policy has helped propel for so long.

The U.S. has inherited and maintained the status quo of a Muslim world divided by colonial European powers. The U.S. maintains complex sets of bilateral and multilateral relations with Muslim-majority states, which are ruled for the most part by rulers who have marginalized civil society. Yet supporters of this untenable relationship are the most vocal in demanding that Muslims, who are rendered powerless, turn inward and band together in order to uproot terrorists.

To state this clearly, it seems contradictory for America to deprive Muslims from governing themselves and then to hold them responsible for mischief that results from them losing control (or genuine sovereignty) over their own lives. Yet Islamic activists across the globe condemned 9/11 in no ambiguous manner. American Muslim leaders and major Islamic centers signed on an anti-terror *fatwa* (religious opinion) issued by major Muslim jurists.[5] And Muslim public affairs agencies have maintained regular contacts with law enforcement agencies.

There is a circular cause and effect relationship between Islamophobia and anti-Americanism. Terrorist attacks against Americans are followed by anti-Muslim rhetoric and action. This in turn reinforces anti-American sentiment and provokes a new round of terrorist attacks. For those like Shanta Premawardhana, who seeks to promote reconciliation, it is pointless to ask which of the two phenomena began first. Suffice it to say that there is a positive relationship between the two, namely, as Islamophobia increases, anti-Americanism is strengthened and vice versa.

Bin Laden's stretching the line of logic beyond reason and fact in blaming America is clearly anti-American, just as the justification of the War in Iraq on grounds of 9/11 is Islamophobic. In both cases the rationalization of the attacks is made via ideology-based views on history and world affairs assigning responsibility for events not on the basis of linking actors with actions but on grounds that selectively mix geopolitical analyses and visions with ethnic, religious and/or national affiliations.

DIALOGUE AND REFORM

In practical terms, legitimate grievances must be addressed to dry up the sources of anger. This is not a call for the United States to relinquish its advantageous military and economic positions to appease others. Nor does it mean that governments in Muslim-majority countries should censor speech in order to prove to the American government that they are cracking down on extremism. As Cantori puts it, it means that the American government should work to resolve or, at the very least, refrain from opposing national liberation movements, because this hostility feeds legitimate resentment against it. He cautions, however, that this may not happen so long as the U.S. government is in the grip of those who believe in an imperial America and are willing to even use and/or ignore America's foundational principles of democarcy and human rights as only policy tools.[6]

If there is one thing that all of the presentations have in common, it is the importance of dialogue in exposing myths and forging a solid understanding in order to build a better future. Broad-brush generalizations distort our understanding of one another. Richard Cizik warns Muslims against equating evangelicals with fundamentalist Christians.

Muslims must relate to his plea, because they have complained for so long that Western academics and journalists invented the term fundamentalist Islam and equate its characteristics with profiles of practicing Muslims, equate those with extremists, and extremists with terrorists. Following the Iranian Revolution in 1979 such assumptions were applied to Shia Muslims and following 9/11 it became fashionable to attack Muslims by calling them *Wahhabi* or *Salafi*, as Anwar Ibrahim points out.

Charting the way out of stereotyping and communication based on ignorant profiling, James Jones admonishes Muslims, Christians, and Jews to acknowledge their Abrahamic roots as one strong foundation for communication between all followers of these three religions. Muzammil Siddiqi demonstrates how the Ten Commandments of the Old Testament have corresponding verses in the Qur'an. Siddiqi also quotes texts from various religious scriptures to prove that the golden rule, which simply recommends treating others as one would like to be treated, is a universal principle that offers solid moral ground for peaceful coexistence.

Subscribers to the theory of political realism may think such lofty ideas will not change the nature of international relations, which, in their view, are based on mistrust, power and interest. But those who believe in the free will of human beings may disagree. Indeed, Scott Alexander would call radical "realists" triumphalists bent on subjugating others. Voll and Safi call for a global discourse premised on a shared future. Within this framework, various sub-discourses may prove fruitful.

One conversation should deal with the notion of world domination. Alexander points out that neither the Qur'an nor the Bible justifies domination and oppression. He cites Princeton scholar Richard Bulliet, arguing that Islamic and Christian civilizations are more interlinked than many are prepared to acknowledge.

Another exchange in the global dialogue revolves around interfaith relations. Cizik, a conservative with the National Association of Evangelicals, asserts that conventional feel-good interfaith meetings have run their course and have produced few tangible results. He calls for an engagement that appreciates differences as well as agreements between faith communities. Premawardhana, a liberal with the National Council of Churches, reminds readers that contacts between Muslims and mainline Protestants have gone beyond pleasant exchanges of good ideas and intentions. There have been joint responses to crises, including political alliances to defend civil rights and oppose unjust wars.

A third discussion involves Muslims in the West and the rest of the *ummah* (worldwide community of believers). There are good ideas Western Muslims are sharing with their fellow Muslims across the globe—ideas that may contribute to reform capable of giving hope and blunting radicalism. For example, take Jamal Badawi's differentiation between secularism and secularity. The former is an anti-religion ideology, which Muslims would oppose, whereas the latter is a principle that allows the creation of effective polities, which Muslims may view as good. He argues that the American model of separating church and state follows the secularity concept. If this understanding becomes a basis for political reform in Muslim-majority countries, it would demonstrate that American principles are consistent with Islamic ideals.

Anyway, Islam never sanctioned a church-like structure. It is the whole community that is entrusted with guarding the faith. And religious authority to Muslims is essentially exercised through scholastic activities that find resonance among ordinary Muslims. No people would develop democratic institutions offending their cherished values. Democratization in harmony with Islam would convince many Muslims to join the political process, which in turn would dry up the sources of violence and anti-Americanism.

Ultimately, controlling criminal actions is a task best handled by security agencies. Muslim-majority countries should not only work to curb terrorist activity, but should also guarantee freedom of speech and association so that extremist ideas can be recognized and isolated by mainstream Muslim opinion. This prospect could prove more effective than American military adventures. Only the hope of a better future can temper the frustration of increasingly desperate Muslims.

But there are voices arguing that Muslims are not ready for democracy or that Islam and democratic ideals are not compatible. Anwar Ibrahim posits that the talk of this supposed incompatibility could manifest Islamophobia. Essentially, it suggests that Muslims are prone to violence and prefer war over negotiations to settle their differences. He recommends that American civil society groups engage their counterparts in Muslim-majority states, rather than justify denying them a place at the political table. From this perspective, Ibrahim argues, the debate over Islam and democracy must be seen in a new light: Subscribers to the notion that the two are incompatible are those who would like to see the West clash with the Muslim world. In other words, the question of compatibility is not answerable through a positivist scientific discovery. Rather, it is subject to one's preferences regarding East-West relations. Those who opt for conflict would welcome the intensification of Islamophobia and anti-Americanism.

Yet there is merit to the argument that Muslims must focus on solving serious problems threatening their cultural life and even the very existence of their faith community. There is civil war in Iraq.

Palestinians under Israeli occupation engage in self-ruining factional fighting. And Muslims kill Muslims in Darfur, Sudan.

Obstacles and Catalysts for Change

Serious obstacles limit the chances of a meaningful conversation. Denial is major complicating factor. Claude Selhani shares his experience with a group of Saudi intellectuals who denied that al-Qaidah had a role in 9/11. He reports that they insisted the CIA hatched the attacks to justify the subsequent wars. Such an attitude widens the gap of understanding. Similarly, some Americans deny that Islamophobia exists or that anti-Americanism is related to America's unjustified militarism and support of oppression. Instead, they claim that Muslims hate America for its freedom and democracy. Public opinion polls in the Muslim world conducted by Western pollsters debunk this Islamophobic myth. The most recent of such surveys was conducted by the Program on International Policy Attitudes in April 2007. It shows that majorities in Morocco, Egypt, Pakistan, and Indonesia, four heavily populated Muslim-majority countries in North Africa, the Middle East, South Asia, and Southeast Asia, oppose attacks on civilians, support the application of Islamic law in their countries, favor democratic governance, and see value in openness to global exchange.[7]

Another impediment is condescending attitudes toward others, which eliminate the prospects of building what Alexander calls the "relationships of trust" necessary for a fruitful engagement. Muslims who speak of America as a sick culture contribute to the reinforcement of mistrust. Members of Congress, like Virgil Goode (R-VA), who objected to the preference of Keith Ellison (D-MN), a fellow legislator, to take his oath on the Qur'an, reinforce Muslim fear of exclusionary politics.

The media, often the venue transmitting tolerant and intolerant speech, are often accused of promoting stereotypes that feed prejudice. However, media outlets and professionals vary in performance—some are more culturally competent than others. The political and ideological interests feeding them are too diverse; they cannot be lumped together. Hafiz al-Mirazi contends that charges of anti-Americanism against Al-Jazeera are politically motivated and loaded with double standards. He offers the example of its coverage of angry reactions to news about American soldiers flushing the Qur'an down a toilet at the American detention center in Guantánamo Bay, Cuba. American officials accused the satellite television station of hyping anti-American sentiment. This charge, however, was not leveled against *Newsweek*, the original source of the news. Nor were American television stations criticized for carrying reports of demonstrations against the offensive act.

The media should not be censored on account of having some bad players. However, media personnel should be educated so that all false, unsubstantiated, and taken-out-of-context coverage is replaced by treatment based on sourced facts. Besides the media, academia can benefit from such reform. Scholars are entrusted with educating the public about complex issues. When they choose, instead, to justify the acts of their preferred political and religious leaders, they betray the very function of knowledge production with which society has entrusted them.

Yet, conservative weblogs along with the often labeled "liberal" entertainment industry tend to reinforce very negative stereotypes about Muslim religious and political groups. Such portrayals may sometimes result from the producers' own ignorance. Jones, however, contends that the negative labeling of others is usually intended to stigmatize and downgrade them for the purpose of social and political control.

Some columnists and "scholars" make use of such labels for the purpose of influencing public opinion and public policy. Neoconservative pundit Frank Gaffney speaks of "moderate Muslims" as "courageous, heroic and often alone."[8] He wants to have it both ways: to be seen as someone who is only against "Islamists" not "Islam"[9] and to persuade Americans that there are only a few isolated moderate Muslims who could be liked. So in the mind of this Islamophobe, the moderate label is only a convenient cover for his vilification of Muslims.

Opinion leaders share some blame. Samer Shehata demonstrates how talk-show hosts and divisive religious leaders may have a vested interest in harsh rhetoric. Extremist speech can be effective in rallying support, and extremists have no incentive to change unless their ways are repudiated. When they are challenged by mainstream leaders, they tend to tone down their rhetoric. Talk-show hosts have even apologized in public when their divisive speech began to threaten their financial support base. In general, such repudiation is rare, and thus divisive opinion leaders shoulder some responsibility for provoking mutually reinforcing cycles of Islamophobia and anti-Americanism.

Exploring reconciliation takes the conversation to the group with the highest stakes in this endeavor: American Muslims. Cherrif Bassiouni believes that American Muslims have a great potential of becoming the catalyst for meaningful dialogue, because they are both Muslim and American. While resisting marginalization, they should fight extremism by engaging others constructively and striving to build on the great values of Islam and America. Asma Afsaruddin offers testimony showing that American Muslims are attempting to meet this challenge through their work and personal lives.

THE CHALLENGES
OF DEFINING ISLAMOPHOBIA
AND ANTI-AMERICANISM

Prejudice is Real and Exacts a Heavy Toll

Parvez Ahmed

ISLAMOPHOBIA REFERS TO unfounded fear of and hostility towards Islam. Such fear and hostility leads to discrimination against Muslims, exclusion of Muslims from mainstream political or social process, stereotyping, the presumption of guilt by association, and finally hate crimes. In twenty-first century America, all of these evils are present and in some quarters tolerated. While America has made major progress in racial harmony, there is still a long road ahead of us to reach our destination when all people are judged on the content of their character and neither on the color of their skin or their faith.

Islamophobia as a term and as a phenomenon gained currency in part due to the popular thesis developed by Samuel Huntington that argued about an impending clash of civilization between Islam and the West. When 9-11 happened, the people already predisposed to viewing Islam with suspicion jumped on this bandwagon and through a multitude of primarily right wing outlets have been successful in creating a climate of extreme prejudice, suspicion and fear against Muslims. This sentiment has also been aided by many pro-Israeli commentators such as Daniel Pipes, Steve Emerson, Judith Miller, and Bernard Lewis among many others.

Islamophobia has resulted in the general and unquestioned acceptance of the following:

- Islam is monolithic and cannot adapt to new realities.
- Islam does not share common values with other major faiths.

- Islam as a religion is inferior to the West. It is archaic, barbaric and irrational.
- Islam is a religion of violence and supports terrorism.
- Islam is a violent political ideology. [10]

Under such assumptions any criticism by Muslims of American policy towards the Muslim world is dismissed as being "reactionary," "anti-Semitic" and "irrational." Mainstream American Muslim organizations are viewed with suspicion and a variety of excuses are put forward for not engaging the American Muslim community.

Such biased attitudes are present despite the fact that Muslim contributions played a significant part in developing a civilization in Europe, and history books record the first Muslim arrival in America in 1312 when Mansa Abu Bakr traveled from Mali to South America. Additionally, of the estimated 10 million African slaves that came to America a significant percentage was Muslim.[11] Yet Islam and Muslims remain in Europe and America embedded in stereotypical assumptions and misguided pronouncements regarding beliefs, attitudes and customs.

In 2006 the Council on American-Islamic Relations (CAIR) commissioned a survey of American Muslim voters. Results show that American Muslim voters are young, highly educated, (62 percent have obtained a bachelor degree or higher. This is double the comparable national figure for registered voters), more than half the community is made up of professionals, 43 percent have a household income of $50,000 or higher, 78 percent are married and the community is religiously diverse (31 percent attend a mosque on a weekly basis; 16 percent attend once or twice a month; 27 percent said they seldom or never attend). The largest segment of the respondents said they consider themselves "just Muslims," avoiding distinctions like Sunni or Shia. Another 36 percent said they are Sunni and 12 percent said they are Shia. Less than half of 1 percent said they are Salafi, while 2 percent said they are Sufi.[12]

The survey results also show, that American Muslims are integrated in American society—89 percent said they vote regularly; 86 percent said they celebrate the Fourth of July; 64 percent said they fly the U.S. flag; 42 percent said they volunteer for institutions serving the public (compared to 29 percent nationwide in 2005). On social and political issues the views of American Muslims are as follows: 84 percent said Muslims should strongly emphasize shared values with Christians and Jews, 82 percent said terrorist attacks harm American Muslims; 77 percent said Muslims worship the same God as Christians and Jews do; 69 percent believe a just resolution to the Palestinian cause would improve America's standing in the Muslim world; 66 percent support working toward normalization of relations with Iran; 55 percent are afraid that the War on Terror has become a war on Islam; only 12 percent believe the war in Iraq was a worthwhile effort; and just 10 percent support the use of the military to spread democracy in other countries.[13]

Despite such integrative attitudes, the rise of anti-Muslim sentiment in the U.S. creates tensions and hinders quicker integration of Muslims. Here are some of the recent results of American public attitude towards Islam and Muslims:

• The Pew Forum on Religion and Public Life Poll in 2004:
– Almost 4 in 10 Americans have an unfavorable view of Islam, about the same number that has a favorable view.
– A plurality of Americans (46 percent) believes that Islam is more likely than other religions to encourage violence among its believers.[14]

• Cornell University December 2004 Poll:

– In all, about 44 percent said they believe that some curtailment of civil liberties is necessary for Muslim Americans.

– Twenty-six percent said they think that mosques should be closely monitored by U.S. law enforcement agencies.

– Twenty-nine percent agreed that undercover law enforcement agents should infiltrate Muslim civic and volunteer organizations, in order to keep tabs on their activities and fund raising.[17]

• ABC News March 2005 Poll:

– Four months after 9/11, 14 percent believed mainstream Islam encourages violence; today it's 34 percent.

– Today 43 percent think Islam does not teach respect for the beliefs of non-Muslims—up sharply from 22 percent.

– People who feel they do understand Islam are much more likely to view it positively. Among Americans who feel they do understand the religion, 59 percent call it peaceful and 46 percent think it teaches respect for the beliefs of others.[15]

• CAIR 2005 Poll on American Attitudes Towards Islam and Muslims:

– The level of knowledge of Islam is virtually unchanged from 2004. Only two percent of survey respondents indicated that they are "very knowledgeable" about the religion.

– Almost 60 percent said they "are not very knowledgeable" or "not at all knowledgeable" about Islam.

– Nearly 10 percent said Muslims believe in a moon god.

– Just a little over one-third of survey respondents reported awareness of Muslim leaders condemning terrorism.

– A vast majority of Americans said they would change their views about Muslims if Muslims condemn terrorism more strongly, show more concern for Americans or work to improve the status of Muslim women or American image in the Muslim world.[16]

Such public atmosphere translates into discrimination, exclusion and violence. In 2006, CAIR processed a total of 2,467 civil rights complaints, compared to 1,972 in 2005 and 1,522 in 2004.[18] This constitutes a 62 percent increase in the total number of complaints of anti-Muslim harassment, violence and discriminatory treatment from 2004. For the third straight year, the 2,467 reports also mark the highest number of Muslim civil rights complaints ever reported to CAIR in its thirteen-year history. In addition, CAIR received 167 reports of anti-Muslim hate crime complaints in 2006, an 18 percent increase from the 141 complaints received in 2004.

The impact of Islamophobia is not only seen in these large increases in complaints of discrimination by Muslims but it can have other consequences that will be very detrimental to the overall society. Muslim youth in the West have grown up being preached ideas of plurality, equality and freedom. When such ideas are not applied towards their own empowerment it can lead to disillusionment, social disorder and in the worst cases irrational violence.

Islamophobia also weakens the American social fabric. The presence of an educated, professional and patriotic class of American Muslims ought to be viewed as a resource and strength as they can greatly aid in improving America's image in the Muslim world. American Muslims have deep appreciation and love for America just as they have empathy and understanding of the Muslim world. Thus

American Muslims can serve as the perfect bridge between America and the Muslim world. To enable this aspiration, American policy makers need to constructively engage American Muslims. American Muslim representation within most policy making circles (congressional or executive) is almost non-existent. Islamophobia prevents meaningful engagement with Muslims as politicians using the calculus of votes and money play it safe by caving into the tyranny of the majority.

The way forward is to develop a sense of urgency that Islamophobia ought to be made unacceptable just as racism and anti-Semitism are in America. Islamophobia is already beginning to erode America's image and culture. Opinion leaders should view Islam, a faith with diversity, internal differences, having much in common with Christianity and Judaism, as distinctly different but not deficient, and as a partner in America's future.

TRUTH AND VANITY SHAPE ANTI-AMERICANISM AND ISLAMOPHOBIA

Louay Safi

NTI-AMERICANISM AND Islamophobia share a common denominator: Both are used as strategic weapons in the war of ideas, particularly among people who stand on radical sides of the political/ideological spectrum, both in Muslim societies and in the United States. On one level we can recognize that both anti-Americanism and Islamophobia stem from the misrepresentations, ignorance, lies, and half-truths put out by American extremists on the far Right. We see how these people are bent on delivering an ideological message to defame Islam and marginalize Muslims.

But on a deeper level, both stem from a very basic human instinct: the will to power. This includes the very basic human follies of greed; and the desire to control, expand, and dominate. It is important to recognize that while some sources are superficial, there are other—and real—forces behind those sentiments. We have to deal with them.

When we explore these two sentiments, we have to also look at two other notions, American foreign policy and terrorism, both of which have contributed to the rise of anti-Americanism and Islamophobia. The most interesting thing is that these two notions are not completely independent; rather, they are interrelated. American foreign policy has given rise to terrorism, and terrorism is pushing American policy more toward creating anti-Americanism throughout the world. These sentiments are not particular to Muslims. For example, one can find them among South Americans who have experienced American foreign policy and this country's heavy hand when dealing with outside forces. Similar sentiments can be found in Europe and Asia. The Pew Survey, a very rich source of information, reveals the extent of the resentment and critical views toward American foreign policy.

Both truth and vanity shape the sentiments of anti-Americanism and Islamophobia. I am not very concerned about those sources that stem from human vanity. We can think of jealousy as a source of anti-Americanism, which many of this country's leaders have cited many times. Perhaps part of that is true, based on the fact that the United States is a superpower that is trying to shape world politics. Naturally, such power is resented.

But this is not the source of my worry. I am concerned about those elements that come out of truth, not out of vanity. We should be particularly concerned with American foreign policy that intends to extend or expand American interests at the expense of other societies' dignity and well-being. I am also concerned about the exclusivist ideologies spreading throughout the Muslim world and this country, ideologies that want to set one group against the other. As American Muslims, we have to pay attention to these aspects.

Those among us who are following the Bush administration's statements, as well as the president's, have probably recognized that there has been a shift in the discourse and its statements, a shift toward emphasizing and recognizing the importance of democracy as well as the importance of this country standing behind popular movements that are furthering democracy and freedom and opposing dictatorial and oppressive regimes. This is a welcome and important change. Those of us who have seen foreign policy advanced by political realism know that the Bush administration's foreign policy has been very cynical. Policymakers have been emphasizing America's national interests and saying that we cannot talk about morality beyond our borders. In a world where communication and transportation have become so advanced that a sense of togetherness has been created, in a world where globalism and globalization has advanced, we need a new shift in the way we think about one another, in the way that one political society thinks about another political society.

There must be a change from a society where one class can claim privileges and sees fit to manipulate and exploit other classes and segments of society, to a society in which no one would dare to stand up and say: "I can advance my interests and the interests of my neighbors at the expense of everybody else, and if you don't like it you have to live with it."

When we listen to most political leaders who adhere to or espouse political realism, we hear them telling us that we, as a nation, can exploit other nations because doing so is natural. They suggest that every nation has to look after its own interests, even if that means national interests expressed in terms of geopolitics and economics, even if our interests have to be advanced at the expense of the Egyptians, Syrians, Brazilians, or Indians. This is not right and must change. We can and should play a role in that. It is a high order, but it is something we can accomplish if our community starts thinking big and starts preparing itself for that role.

We know that with the coming of the neoconservatives and their doctrine of military preeminence, real political thinking has not changed.

What we have been given is another version of foreign policy, one in which we talk about the advance of democracy and freedom throughout the world. I cannot count how many times George Bush has repeated the word freedom. It is a key word in his discourse. The second aspect of this new doctrine is that we, as a nation, have to ensure that we always enjoy military superiority in order to dominate.

But what happens when our desire and push to dominate conflicts with our mission of advancing freedom and democracy throughout the world? Which interest gets the priority? The second always will. Our dominance always comes before our mission to advance democracy. This used to be called the doctrine of selective engagement. In the past, we were taught that we are for democracy and our national interests, but that we cannot police the world. Ultimately, this means that we have to be selective in our engagements and promotion of democracy. Somehow this always happens when we want to control and dominate another society.

What should American Muslims do about the serious challenges facing us, such as anti-Americanism at the same time we suffer from Islamophobia, which is hurting us tremendously? First of all, we need to build and strengthen our communities. We have to ensure that more American Muslims are engaged in public discourse, that we speak on issues and are part of the political process. In addition to voting, American Muslims should run for Congress and those who are journalists should participate in the media.

We also have to serve as a bridge between the Muslim world and the West. This will not be achieved by simply volunteering to be part of the public diplomacy exercise. In fact, doing so could burn all of us if we appear as people who seek to advance policies that are harmful to other societies. We have to participate in public diplomacy. We should attempt to gain a greater understanding of American society and its diversity. In addition, we should try to explain to people in the Muslim world that not all Americans are neoconservatives obsessed with domination. Moreover, we have to play our role and be honest spokespersons for the rights and dignity of people belonging to other societies, particularly those Muslim societies that are suffering as a result of the global configuration.

Ultimately, what matters is how American Muslims behave and work on the ground, not necessarily the phobia of anti-Islam forces in this country. For example, Daniel Pipes, a major Islamophobe, was rebuked by the entire board of the United States Institute of Peace (USIP) in March 2004, when he tried using lies, half-truths, and innuendoes to marginalize and push away the Center for the Study of Islam and Democracy, an Islamic organization that was working with USIP. Sooner or later, such Islamophobes will be exposed when the facts become known.

What matters are the organizations, like the one attacked by Pipes, that are engaged in constructive efforts. We need to emphasize their good work and not the Islamophobes. Some of us, from time to time, will have to confront these Islamophobes. But we must remain focused on building our community and getting involved in different aspects of American society.

As Muslims, we have to realize that the values of pluralism, freedom of religion, and mutual respect—the foundations of democracy—are values that Muslims share. Therefore, we should never hesitate to say that Islam and democracy are compatible. In fact, I cannot see democracy being established in Muslim societies without Islam playing a leading role. To undergo the transformation toward democracy, very strong and deep commitments are needed. And these can only come from religious convictions. They cannot come from a cost-benefit analysis.

Democracy is not just about the process of voting. Rather, it is about a set of values that recognizes the right of others to participate in the process, along with the recognition of all people's dignity. We can disagree with one another and with the neo-conservatives, but we have to recognize that they have the right to express themselves politically. Let's speak back to them, clarifying where they are confused, where they are going wrong, and where they are lying.

CHARGING OPPONENTS WITH ANTI-AMERICANISM IS OLD POLITICS

John Voll

MY GREAT GRANDFATHER thought European wars were stupid, so he brought his sons and his wife from Germany (Prussia) to the United States. He maintained the view that European wars were ill-advised and wasteful while he lived in America. During the First World War, those views brought trouble to the generation of his sons, when many German-Americans opposed the entry of the United States into a European war. When "the United States entered the war against Germany in 1917, people were swept into a strong wave of anti-German hysteria. Citizens of German origin were individually harassed and persecuted, and serious efforts were made to eliminate German language and culture in the United States."[19] In an area like central Wisconsin, where my father's family is from, there was a large community of German immigrants and they were subject to "the anti-German hysteria that swept the country after the United States had declared war."[20]

The second generation of people accused of anti-Americanism in my family was my father's generation. He was a Methodist minister in rural Wisconsin in the years between the First and the Second World Wars, at a time of agricultural depression and extreme unemployment. My father was also a farmer's union organizer and often supported Christian socialist ideas and policies. By the time of the Cold War between the United States and the Soviet Union began, people like my father were often viewed as threats to American security and were accused of being communists or communist sympathizers. As a Methodist minister he was part of an occupational group that was suspected by the House Un-American Activities Committee (U. S. Congress) and other anti-communist activists in the 1940's and 1950s. A famous article in 1953 written by J. B. Mathews, who was on the staff of the Congressional com-mittee of Senator Joseph McCarthy, asserted that "the largest single group supporting the Communist apparatus in the United States today is composed of Protestant clergymen."[21] The charges of anti-Americanism were especially vigorously debated in the Methodist Church because many Methodist clergy strongly advocated of programs emphasizing social justice and economic equality. This was seen by anti-communist activists as being sympathetic to communism.[22]

The third generation of accusations of anti-Americanism began when I started teaching at the University of New Hampshire in the mid-1960s. The rest of the country had gotten rid of Senator Joseph McCarthy, but New Hampshire still had people who strongly believed even conservative and Republican New Hampshire was infiltrated by communists. The University of New Hampshire was, of course, believed by these people to be filled with communist intellectuals and sympathiz-ers. In the early 1960s, one professor invited a Marxist scholar to give a lecture on campus, and there was significant pressure on the University administration to fire that professor. Some of these activities thought to be subversive were supporting the New Hampshire World Affairs Council, especially its Great Decisions Program. The major newspaper in the state, The Manchester Union Leader, strongly opposed such programs and activities as being anti-American. These were programs in which I participated. So here is my confession: I am associated with three generations of activities that some types of extremists view as being anti-American.

We are looking for answers to the question "What should be the role of Muslims and Muslim organizations?" I would like to broaden the scope of the question to include me: "What should be the role of people like us who are accused by some of being anti-American?" We need to step back and really think about this subject. Much of the discussion in America has been a discussion of anti-Americanism "out there." "Why do they hate us?" and "Why should we fear them?" Questions like these are common and they keep the subject at a distance.

Part of the difficulty and danger in this issue is that real anti-Americanism often creates broadly defined responses. This provides at least some of the roots of Islamophobia as it has developed in the West in recent years. This is not a unique phenomenon. In broader terms, Americans have at times exhibited a deeply engrained public phobia about possible anti-Americanism. The result is a paranoid ideology of anti-"anti-Americanism."

Anything that can be labeled anti-American (whether correctly or wrongly) is what the anti-"anti-Americans" will oppose. One finds elements of this anti-"anti-Americanism" going all the way back to the Alien and Sedition Acts passed in 1798, through the Red Scares in 1919-1920 to the hunts for communists and communist sympathizers by Senator McCarthy and others in the Cold War era. What can possible objects of this phobia of anti-"anti-Americanism" do? This can be called anti-squared Americanism (anti2-Americanism). What can we do about anti2- Americanism?

There are two kinds of phobias that are confused with each other. It is important to distinguish between them. These two might be distinguished as anti-"un-Americanism" and anti-"anti-Americanism." These different visions, antagonisms, and fears have been aimed at a broad spectrum of peoples with a wide range of identities.

Anti-"un-Americanism" is a negative part of the long history of defining and affirming an "American" national identity. This attitude starts with a basic definition of what it means to be "American," and then views anyone who does not fit within that definition as being foreign and un-American. The "un-American" is some one who is different from the self-defined American mainstream. By the middle of the nineteenth century this definition of America was presented in an enduring historical narrative of the foundations of "American culture." The continuing power of this narrative is shown by the fact that even at the beginning of the twenty-first century it could be re-presented by an influential scholar, Samuel Huntington, in a major intellectual journal. Huntington asserts: "America was created by 17th- and 18th-century settlers who were overwhelmingly white, British, and Protestant. Their values, institutions, and culture provided the foundation for and shaped the development of the United States in the following centuries."[23] During the 19th century, people from other parts of Europe with different religious affiliations became a part of American society. However, Huntington argues that the basic political and social "creed" that "most Americans" see as "the crucial element of their national identity" is "the product of the distinct Anglo-Protestant culture of the founding settlers." [24]

This basic identity narrative provides the foundation for defining the "un-Americans." From the early days of the Republic, Roman Catholics were mistrusted as being un-American and in many states could not legally hold political positions until well into the nineteenth century. The Protestant nature of this identity influenced Presidential elections and many thought that a Catholic could not be elected to the office of President. The election of John F. Kennedy in 1960 illustrated that it could happen, although it did not eliminate anti-Catholic prejudice in the United States.

The "Anglo" dimension of the identity also caused tensions as Europeans from many different countries came to the States. Each group was in some way considered un-American as they came into the country. Among the most important of these groups were the Irish, the Italians, and the Germans. The narrative, and to a large extent the actual historical experiences of these groups was that they became "American" through the power of the "American melting pot." However, the "melting pot" experience in many ways assumed that the way people became "American" was by becoming like the basic Anglo-Protestant pattern. In addition, there were groups that were so different from the mythic mainstream "American" that they were "unmeltable." The Chinese laborers who came as construction workers in the nineteenth century could not assimilate into being "White Anglo-Saxon Protestants (WASPs)." The major group not incorporated into the myth was the African American population, even though they were part of the building of the earliest American settlements and societies. The whole tradition of slavery and its aftermath in the United States placed black Americans in a different category.

The anti-"un-American" tradition is strong. It is a tradition of mistrust and dislike toward peoples who are different and do not fit the mythic definition of "American" that had developed in the nineteenth century. These people were and are viewed as a threat to the nature of "American" culture. It is a cultural phobia or fear that "un-Americans" will dilute and then destroy the Anglo-Protestant culture, which is believed to be the essential foundation for United States society.

This phobia is different from the fears involved in anti-"anti-

Americanism." The "un-Americans" were not viewed as a security threat to the United States. However, at various times in the history of the United States, some in the WASP mainstream came to identify specific groups as possible military or security threats to America. These are the people who were charged, persecuted, or harassed because they were thought to be "anti-American." The most important of these groups were the Germans in World War I, the Japanese in World War II, and, in ideological terms, anybody who was leftist or communist in the era of the Cold War. The "anti-American" label was often frequently used to describe those who opposed the increasing American military involvement in Vietnam.

Anti-"un-Americanism" involved discrimination and prejudice, but anti-"anti-Americanism" sometimes involved direct persecution. During World War I, Germans were convicted of seditious acts and imprisoned simply for saying that the United States should not get involved in the war against Prussia.[25] Thousands of Americans of Japanese origin were interned in concentration camps during World War II.

The history of Muslims in the United States can be viewed in terms of the changing status of the nature of prejudices toward them. Initially, discrimination against Muslims was basically anti-"un-Americanism." The anti-Muslim sentiments of the 1920's through the 1950's were anti-Muslim because Muslims were different, but nobody thought that any Muslim was going to conquer America or that there was an "Islamic threat." However, the situation has changed dramatically in the past decade.

There has been an important transition from mistrust of Muslims because they are different, somehow "un-American," to viewing Muslims as anti-American and a threat to American security. This change can be seen as an important aspect of the rise of Islamophobia in the United States and militant Muslim activism in the world. This process is related in many ways to the world in which we live. Muslim Americans have had very little involvement in the actual anti-American activities that have taken place in the last decade. The actual threats to American interests involve international and transnational crises and have little to do with domestic American affairs. Yet, anti-"anti-Americanism" makes substantial and basically unsupported claims about the threats to American security from American Muslims. These claims rest on alleged ties between Muslim Americans and non-American militant Muslim groups.

The outside world has many conflicts. There is a long-standing relationship between outside conflicts involving American interests and internal American phobias about "anti-Americanism." It becomes important to recognize that one of the best things we can do to cope with Islamophobia and anti-squared Americanism in the United States, is the work to resolve the global conflicts. It does not mean that if the Palestinians and the Israelis can produce a successful peace arrangement, that Americans will stop having phobias. It does provide a way, however, to reduce the sources of Islamophobic attitudes.

In terms of what Americans of all identities can do, one suggestion that I have is that sometimes it is important to recognize shared experiences and common interests. While the contemporary experiences of Muslim Americans are distinctive, it is important not to get buried in an exceptionalism that makes it difficult to work with others. At least some of the issues that are raised by Islamophobia and anti-"anti-Americanism," are issues that families like mine with its three generations of alleged anti-Americanism share with Muslim Americans. There are common grounds for working to create a more open and pluralist sense of American identity, in which difference is neither un-American nor anti-American. Even within the tensions of our current global village, there can be a sense of community.

MISCONCEPTIONS

AMERICA AND THE MUSLIM WORLD MUST CHANGE THEIR LOVE-HATE RELATIONSHIP

Anwar Ibrahim

SINCE THE END of the Second World War, the Muslim world has had a love-hate relationship with the United States. To its detractors, America is the villain with the grand design of global domination, a big bully who preaches democracy through firepower. To its admirers, America is a white knight defending humanity against tyranny. It is also Santa Claus, doling out economic and financial aid. Either way, it is clear that this ambivalent relationship has more to do with money, power, and politics than with religion, culture, or civilization.

Yet, Islamophobia and anti-Americanism continue to dominate our cultural and political discourse. In early May 2005, I addressed a group of university students in London on "Democracy and Terrorism: The Challenges to and Responses of Islam and Human Rights." A useful title, I thought. I wasted no time in alluding to the use of the terms democracy and terrorism being used in the context of Islam and human rights. Juxtaposing these terms evokes a powerful but negative message: It suggests that democracy is diametrically opposed to Islam and that Islam and terrorism are blood brothers, while human rights are the black sheep of the family.

Is this symptomatic of Islamophobia? The question may be bluntly put, but this was clearly part of the stereotyping that has become popular in social currents. It is true that democracy and terrorism are worlds apart. They are as close to each other as Paradise and Hell. While democracy is associated with the rule of law, terrorism is invariably linked to the rule of violence. Democracy liberates humanity and gives people freedom, equality, and the solutions of civil society. Terrorism holds people hostage and gives them fear and uncertainty. So what remains in history is why should democracy not be the backbone of Islamic societies as well? In that regard, political discourses have fallen prey to the ravages of Islamophobia. As I understand it, Islamophobia is the irrational fear of Islam or Muslims, subsumed on the belief that they are religious fanatics who hate non-Muslims.

In an attempt to analyze this phobia, many scholars are ever ready to jump on the *Salafiyyah* (a twentieth-century movement adhering to the writings and practices of the early Muslim interpreters of the Qur'an) bandwagon. They will, of course, go back to the eighth century when fundamentalism, as they term it, was born. The usual suspects are dogmatic rigidity, religious purism, radicalism, Wahhabism, and so on.

Another Islamophobic view appears in the contention that Islam does not separate the secular from the spiritual, that religion is never separated from the state. Leaders who are Islamists will impose Shari'ah law on the people, while secular leaders will make its rejection an essential item of their platform. The former will be considered fundamentalist and backward, while the latter will be hailed as moderate, progressive, and democratic.

My first response to this analysis is that such theoretical generalizations are not grounded in reason and are neither persuasive nor fruitful. *Shari'ah* law is not necessarily outdated or bad, and not all bad laws come from it. Islam is a dynamic religion. The concept of *taqlid* (following the legal opinions of a qualified religious scholar) can leave the door of *ijtihad* (reinterpretation based on the spirit of the scripture) open. Muslim leaders should break free of sloganeering and attempting to establish a utopian Islamic state. Instead, they should get on with the task of governing. An ideal Islamic society includes free speech, freedom from corruption, social justice, and women's rights.

Islamophobia takes on a harsher face in America because of anti-Americanism and the events of 9/11. We should work toward dialogue with other groups. Leaders focus on anti-Americanism in the Muslim world to divert attention from their failed policies and governance. Yet they spend millions on American think tanks to promote regimes that are against democracy and freedom. Therefore charges of anti-Americanism are used as a device to bolster authoritarian rule. Civil liberties are withdrawn. Oppressive laws in the Muslim world hinder democracy. The separation of powers and checks and balances are important.

Let's focus on the ties that bind us, rather than on those things that separate us. Let's turn a deaf ear to those who continue to beat the drums of discord. Let's take the road not taken. Islamophobia and anti-Americanism are not about to vanish overnight. But I believe, God willing, that if we walk through this storm together, there will be a tomorrow to wake up for; a tomorrow in which our minds will be free of the shackles of historical influence and cultural conditions; in which Islam and democracy will converge; in which terrorism and extremism will have no place; and in which we will embrace freedom, human rights, and civil society.

WE SHOULD DECONSTRUCT OUR SUPREMACIST MASTER NARRATIVES

Scott C. Alexander

I WOULD LIKE to offer an analogical metaphor that might help shed some light on the nature of Islamophobia in contemporary Western societies, particularly in the United States. It is important to emphasize that a similar analysis could and should, mutatis mutandis, be undoubtedly applied to the nature of anti-American rhetoric in the Muslim world. Convinced, however, that sincere self-criticism is what is called for in both cases, I will leave this task to my Muslim colleagues living overseas.

The metaphor I have in mind is designed to demonstrate the degree to which Islamophobia is embedded within the larger discourse of one of the West's *supremacist master narratives*.[26] Such narratives are those grand myths of cultural superiority—often centering around religious identity, but by no means exclusively or essentially religious—that, for example, have been nurtured for centuries in both Western Christian and Muslim contexts, as societies in these contexts have told "the story" of how their respective civilizations have related and continue to relate to one another.

I should note at the outset, however, that when I use this concept of the *supremacist master narrative*, I do not do so in a politically and morally naïve way. I am well aware of the fact that any such master narrative in the hands of an economically and technologically dominant party functions in qualitatively different ways, and thus bears an equally different moral status, than when such narratives are used by a party struggling to liberate itself from the oppression of a dominant civilizational "other." In other words, depending on significant power differentials, no two supremacist master narratives are moral equivalents.

In addition to presenting and briefly interpreting my analogical metaphor, I would also like, by way of conclusion, to name and briefly comment upon at least two essential components of any comprehensive strategy for deconstructing our supremacist master narratives. I do so in the interest of building an ideational foundation for peace in the form of a more accurate mutual understanding.

The Metaphor

The metaphor came to me in the form of a story that I heard from Susan O'Halloran,[27] a professional storyteller who grew up on the south side of Chicago in the 1960s as a second-generation Irish Catholic. As an Irish Catholic, she was aware that her grandparents had sacrificed a great deal to come to the United States. She had heard stories of the hardships they had faced, and was very proud of the fact that her family had "made it" in their new home—the only home she ever knew. She and her family did not have it easy, but they did not live in poverty either, at least not any more. She told me that roughly once a month she, her aunt, and her mother would take the elevated train from the south side, where she lived, to the Loop in downtown Chicago. They would do some window-shopping, and every once in a while, when they could afford it, would actually buy something that they needed for a special occasion.

She says that one of the most memorable moments of the journey downtown was when they would pass over the African-American ghettos on the south side. As they passed above the rooftops, these white Irish Catholics literally and metaphorically *looked down* through the smudged windows of the elevated train upon this African-American community, a community with which she and her family had had no first-hand experience whatsoever. This chasm of space and experience, however, did not keep them from passing judgment on it. Although no one put it this way, everyone assumed that he or she had enough information to pass judgment based on what they thought they knew by gazing from their peculiar vantage point.

But what did they know? What did they see? They saw dilapidated houses in various states of disrepair: paint peeling, porches collapsing, boarded and broken windows in almost each and every unit. And even more revolting was the sight of heaps of rotting garbage in every backyard. Each time they witnessed this sight, my friend heard a familiar oral refrain, words that I myself had overheard when I was growing up in an Italian-American community outside of Boston and would hear people talk about the "colored" neighborhoods: "Why do *these people* want to live like this? Don't *they* have any self-respect? After all, we grew up poor, but we weren't dirty. Being poor doesn't mean you have to be filthy. How can *they* expect help from others when they don't even help themselves? You know the old saying: 'God helps those...'."

Had it not been for an extraordinary experience that my Irish Catholic storyteller friend had had during her freshman year at an all-girls Catholic high school on the south side, this refrain would have become the unassailable foundation of her adult (mis)understanding of the African-American community. Early in the fall semester of her freshman year, she met two Catholic religious women (i.e., nuns) who were on fire with the fervor of the Second Vatican Council and therefore deeply committed to ministries centering upon the Church's teachings regarding social justice and the dignity of every human person.

One of these women worked in the African-American community

and offered to take some of the girls with her to a town meeting where they would learn about the struggles of their black "sisters and brothers." Given the negative perspective about African Americans that she was piecing together for herself from her many rides above the ghetto in the elevated train, this young Irish Catholic girl said that she was ambivalent about going. Yet something was drawing her to go with this young nun she admired into a community that she was being taught to fear and abhor. So she went.

She said that in the first ten minutes of being at this town meeting, her entire narrative concerning the African-American community—one she had been taught to internalize from the homogenously safe height, distance, and separation of the elevated train and the cultural gulf between her community and the ghetto—began to disintegrate before her very eyes. She discovered that the African-American community had been struggling for ten years to get the city of Chicago to bring garbage collection services to their neighborhoods. The reason why there were heaps of rotting garbage in people's backyards was because the people had no other way of disposing of their refuse. This was unlike the storyteller's own experience, where folks in her neighborhood would take their garbage to the end of the road in time for the weekly city collection.

She also realized that at that time, before the winning of civil rights, African Americans could not get mortgages from banks. As victims of racial discrimination, they were forced to pay high rents to slumlords who took advantage of their tenants' powerlessness and never once thought of reinvesting any of their profits into repairing the wretched properties they leased to people who had few, if any, other housing options. Why should they, when these profiteers had a captive market for homes no white person would ever dream of occupying?

Quite simply, the story of how this Irish Catholic white girl was taught to "understand" the African-American community out of the blind ignorance of her elevated train experience is an apt analogical metaphor for how most people in the West view the Muslim world in general, and particularly the Arab Muslim world. In the broadest sense, people in the West look at the Muslim world from the "safe" distance of their elevated train thousands of miles away. Most have never visited this part of the world, and those few who are able and choose to visit spend their time seeing things like the Sphinx and the Giza pyramids, monuments to a civilization long dead, rather than meeting the living and breathing inhabitants of a dynamic contemporary center of Arab Muslim culture such as Cairo. In either case, most Westerners have never really come to know the societies they think they are seeing through the smudged train windows of their television sets tuned to what is often the disdainful, self-righteous refrain of Fox News coverage.

Like our Irish Catholic storyteller before her epiphany, when Americans and other Westerners gaze "down" upon the Muslim world, we see the effects of the suffering of our fellow human beings. And because we know nothing of its historical causes, we resort to the time-honored explanation for human suffering when there is no clear understanding of its roots: We blame the victim. It must be the color of *their* skin, or the food *they* eat, or the clothes *they* wear, or the language *they* speak, or the religion *they* practice, or some combination of all the things that make *them* different from *us* and that keep *them* from enjoying the life *we* enjoy.

INTERPRETING THE METAPHOR

Allow me to interpret the metaphor in very explicit terms. I have already indicated that the windows of the elevated train represent the television screens of our mass media in the United States. Like those subway windows, our media generally serves both to limit our perspective on and to seal us off from the realities of life in most of the Muslim world. When was the last time there was a prime-time special on the post-colonial rise of repressive secular totalitarian regimes in the Muslim world? How many American families have discussed, over Thanksgiving dinner, the generous financial support these regimes have enjoyed from the West and the effects that these regimes and their policies have had on local economies in the Muslim world? How many of those voters who support current American foreign policy in the Middle East have thought for even a moment that agitation against these regimes and their Western supporters have more to do with these circumstances rather than with some allegedly fatal flaw in Islamic culture?

As for the piles of rotting trash and the dilapidated houses, they are analogous to the state of most of the Muslim countries' economic infra-structures, which are designed to benefit a local elite who live like kings among peasants, as well as a global elite who care little for the effects that their personal or corporate aggrandizement has on the majority of their fellow human beings.

Although I made no overt reference to Chicago City Hall in the story of my Irish Catholic friend, its shadow looms large over the African-American ghetto of those days (and of today, for that matter). Just as Chicago City Hall was unquestionably—especially in those days—a seat of white political power backed by its business patrons with their unrivaled economic wealth, its analogue for our understanding of the Muslim world today are those Western nation states and multinational corporations that together play the role of absentee landlords in this scenario. They essentially extort riches from myriad local economies in the Muslim world for their own gain. Then, if the market so dictates, they think nothing of moving their capital from one struggling economy to another, regardless of the effects that this has on the people who cannot follow the capital. And even when they do stay, these absentee landlords tend to siphon off, for themselves and for a select group of native superintendent cronies, whatever prosperity is to be had from the local economy, thereby leaving the masses in relative or abject poverty.

And just as the legacy of racism and one of its crowning achievements, chattel slavery, provides the indispensable historical framework for understanding how so many African Americans came to live in such poverty in the first place, the legacy of Western colonialism and imperialism in the Muslim world is the historical framework about which few American citizens are aware. However, without such awareness there can be no reasoned and just assessment of the current situation. Of course, what is necessary are honest, intelligent leaders with the courage to show us our mistakes and the vision to chart a way out of the quagmire of antipathy and violence in which we find ourselves. Not that we have come even close to where we should be, but where would American society be today were it not for such prophetic voices of social justice as Frederick Douglass, Harriet Tubman, Rosa Parks, Reverend Dr. Martin Luther King, Jr., and Malcolm X, to name a few, who held up a mirror for us so that we could see just where our sordid past of hideous racism and exploitation had brought us?

Upon reflection, this becomes one of the most sobering elements of our analogical metaphor. Chattel slavery endured in the Americas for a good five centuries. Even after benefiting from the likes of Dr. King and Malcolm X, we are still struggling to outlive its legacy. The same is basically true for Western colonial and imperial domination of the Muslim world. Not only were colonial and imperialist systems in place for at least three centuries in the Muslim world, but, catalyzed by 9/11, it now seems that the history of Western colonial and imperial domination of the Muslim world has entered a pernicious new phase. And yet, in this case, there appears to be a distinct lack of prophetic leadership on both sides of the divide. The Dr. Kings and Malcolm Xs of this scenario apparently have either not yet emerged or are being silenced and/or ignored as soon as they do.

Continuing to interpret the metaphor, we could also assert that the levels and shape of violence in both scenarios (i.e., the inner city and the Muslim world) are also analogous, especially in two important respects. They are analogous in that the economic and political deprivation and marginalization so characteristic of the Muslim world are, like their inner-city counterparts in the first scenario, the breeding ground for the social unrest and violence that are gradually beginning to emerge on a larger and larger scale. They are also analogous in that while the powers that be are by no means immune to this violence (e.g., the assassinations of Sadat and Rabin and the heinous but successful 9/11 attack), those who suffer most are the poor and marginalized masses who have as much control over their own violent agitators as they do over their alien overlords (e.g., the Afghan people in the aftermath of 9/11).

By way of concluding the explicit unpacking of our analogical metaphor, it should be noted that one important place where it breaks down (although *not* in Europe and *not* in the case of African-American Muslims in the United States) is in the case of a large percentage of the immigrant Muslims living in this country. For the most part, these people live under favorable economic conditions due to their relative affluence and levels of educational achievement they have attained since the 1960s.

Although these Muslims have not been marginalized economically, it is critical to note that they are still quite vulnerable. In fact, while they may not experience a significant degree of economic marginalization, they nonetheless experience psychological marginalization on a regular basis. Be they women who have their *hijab* (headcovering) torn off in a local MacDonald's or career professionals who allow their colleagues to call them "Moe" instead of "Muhammad" because the latter is "too difficult to pronounce." These immigrant Muslims and their children live under the Damoclean ultimatum of what I have referred to elsewhere as *civil blackmail*: Certify yourselves as "good Muslims" by your enthusiastic pursuit of assimilation and by either remaining politically silent or actively endorsing American foreign policy (whatever it may be).[28] Or, suffer the consequences of categorization as "bad Muslims" and ready yourself for Guantánamo, "extraordinary rendition," or the very real possibility of a Manzanar redux. [Editor's note: Manzanar is the name of the detention camp in which American citizens of Japanese descent were interned during the Second World War.]

THE FUNCTION OF THE WEST'S SUPREMACIST MASTER NARRATIVES

Through her story, my Irish Catholic friend gives us some insight into how she witnessed and participated in perpetuating a supremacist master narrative by drawing on the very isolated, alienating, and one-sided experiences she was having vis-à-vis the African Americans with whom she shared a city. It is important to note that while she was having these experiences, chattel slavery had formally ended. However, its shameful legacy was still very much alive. The dominant culture continued controlling and marginalizing the African-American community. White domination had by no means faded in the wake of Emancipation; it simply changed its face in order to adapt and survive.

We would be lucky if we could say the same about the relationship between the West and the Muslim world. Indeed, colonialism *per se* and the overt imperialist policies of the European powers may officially be things of the past. By the same token, however, as I alluded to above, many have argued quite reasonably that we have entered a new imperialistic age, an age of Western neo-imperialism where the United States has stepped up to assume the role of the dominant Western empire.

What is the specific function, then, of Western supremacist master narratives in the relationship between the West and the Muslim world? Crucial to the longevity of any society's will-to-power is a common story or narrative that asserts the dominant society's cultural superiority over all others. This is not a new idea. Those who are familiar with the work of the late cultural critic Edward Said and the thesis of his book *Orientalism* (Vintage: 1979) know that much of his work was devoted precisely to exposing these kinds of supremacist master narratives. Of special interest to him were those master narratives developed in the West vis-à-vis the East and, in particular, the Muslim world. For Said, Orientalism was not just an academic discipline, but rather an entire ethos that ultimately portrayed the East as worthy of cultural domination by the West precisely because the former was allegedly inferior to the latter in almost every way imaginable: economically, technologically, philosophically, and, let's not forget, religiously. Once viewed through the lenses of the Orientalist master narrative, it was not only justifiable for the West to dominate the Muslim world, but it could be construed as a moral imperative to do so.

And this is, in fact, how many in the West, especially many of those in the Western Christian missionary movement, saw the situation. In short, the supremacist master narrative was and remains a *sine qua non* of any long-term domination of one people over another because it acts as the source of legitimization for this domination not only within the dominant culture, but, to a certain extent— within the subjugated culture as well.[29]

THE ROLE OF THE BIBLE AND THE QUR'AN

An unfortunate but equally undeniable fact is the central role played by religion, in particular Christianity and Islam, in constructing supremacist master narratives in both the Christian and the Muslim worlds. Indeed, the Bible and the Qur'an have histories of being frequently proof-texted in the interest of bringing divine/ultimate authority to these narratives. Given these histories, Christians and Muslims who wish to rescue their sacred texts from the hands of those who would exploit them to support the domination of one people over another must stand up and be counted. They must point out the many ways in which, while embodying traditions of necessary and just violence in certain sharply circumscribed circumstances (i.e., resisting an otherwise unstoppable oppression and injustice), the Bible and the Qur'an strongly oppose the notion that any one society or community ought to dominate or oppress another. In particular, the Bible and Qur'an stand against those who would claim that there is something inherent in any group identity (be it that of Israel's "chosenness," salvation in the body of Christ, or membership in the *ummah* of Muhammad) that makes its members superior to others.

While many scriptural passages come to mind, the one most prominent for me is that part of a Qur'anic verse that, after alluding to the fact that human cultural diversity is a divine gift, says: "Surely, the most noble among you is the most God-conscious."[30] Notice that the most noble is not the one who belongs to this or that group or who calls himself or herself by this or that name. Here I take the Qur'an to be squarely standing against the politicization of religious identity.

From the Qur'anic and Biblical perspectives, faith compels us to be actively engaged in politics. However, it also warns us never to allow politics to co-opt and corrupt our faith. In other words, politics must serve faith by sanctifying the world through an uncompromising commitment to such universal values as the inalienable dignity of every human being regardless of ethnicity, religion, age, sexuality, or gender. Never should faith be allowed to become, as it has so often in human history, the handmaid of politics, blasphemously lending an aura of divine fiat to any worldly agenda designed to destroy the human family by subjugating certain members of that family to the will of certain other members.

Conclusion: Toward Deconstructing Supermarket Master Narratives

By way of conclusion, allow me to mention just two important components of what must necessarily be a much larger and extremely multifaceted strategy for deconstructing our supremacist master narratives.

First, Jews, Christians, Muslims, and others who are committed to a very different way of interacting culturally and inter-religiously must recognize the need for a critically competent and balanced historiography that accounts especially for the experience of those traditionally demonized or ignored by the master narratives. One of the first casualties in constructing any supremacist master narrative is a memory of the past that allows all voices to be heard and all stories to be told and fairly evaluated. If there is one thing a supremacist master narrative cannot countenance, it is fairness and the pursuit of objectivity. After all, making the argument for supremacy of one over another can hardly indulge any attempt to see the two as equals. Thus, we need to indict and call to account those interpretations of history we encounter—no matter what aura of authority they may have—that serve to legitimize various forms of oppression of one group by another. It is especially important that we do this in our religious schools and other institutions, as well as in our public educational outreach.

The second thing, which perhaps speaks to the heart of our faith traditions more directly, is that we have to eschew what is sometimes referred to as *triumphalism*. Too often, Christians and Muslims especially have been guilty of confusing triumphalism with their commitment to the universal claims of their respective worldviews. It must be argued that triumphalism, which I define as the will to force one's own vision of the world onto others and to subjugate and dominate them in order to propagate that vision, has been the single worst enemy of both the Christian and Muslim claims to universal truth.

The logic here is deceptively simple: If, in the name of my religion, I express a will to dominate and dehumanize the other in any way, the last thing that the other will recognize about the truth I pretend to live is its universality. Therefore, if Christians and Muslims really seek to live the universality of their respective traditions, then we will need to think long and hard about eschewing triumphalism. As for the fact that many, if not most, Christians and Muslims cannot imagine what a non-triumphalist Christianity and Islam might look like, this should not discourage us. Rather, it should be a sobering indication of just how much work lies ahead.

LET US RE-EXAMINE THE CONCEPT OF SECULARISM

Jamal Badawi

ALL PRAISE IS due to Allah, the sole Creator, Sustainer, and Cherisher of the universe. May His peace and blessings be on his last Prophet and Messenger, Muhammad, and upon all his fellow prophets and messengers.

In this introductory invocation, some important common religious values have been raised. First, we acknowledge God, by whatever name we use, *Allah* in Arabic or *Allaha* in Aramaic, which are strikingly similar. He is the sole Creator and Sustainer of the universe, and the only Creator and Preserver of the crown of His creation: the human being. That is perhaps the very basic foundation of any religious value, especially when one is referring to the Abrahamic community. The invocation of peace and salutation on all of the prophets and messengers is a central religious value that we all share. The ultimate and supreme source of guidance would have to come from the Creator Himself.

Should religious values be reasserted, not only in private but also in the public space? What are the parameters of that reassertion? We must ask these questions to eliminate any fears and dangers about the tyranny of the minority, or the tyranny of the majority for that matter. How are we faring in North America? Finally, how can we better address these questions?

Some congressional sessions begin with prayers. A huge Christmas tree is placed in the White House every year. Government and semi-governmental institutions have appointed chaplains, paid in part or in full, directly or indirectly, from taxpayers' money to serve in universities, hospitals, and even in the military establishment. Religious values played a pivotal role in the founding of the United States, and they still do. To the north of the United States' border is Canada, whose charter of rights and freedom signed in 1982 begins with the statement: "Whereas Canada is founded upon the principle that recognizes the supremacy of God and the rule of law...." If we go beyond North America, across the Atlantic to the United Kingdom, we know that its queen or king is the official "defender of the faith," in this case the Anglican faith. On my last trip to the United Kingdom, I was happy to hear Prince Charles say that if he happens to become king, "defender of the faith" will mean all faiths, and not just the Anglican or Christian faith.

Many Western countries are actually based on and influenced by certain religious values that affect their governments. We cannot really make a separation. What happened in most cases is not really a separation between religion and state, but between church and state in the form of institutions. This is perhaps a legacy of medieval European history.

I would like to address two basic guidelines. First, secularism does not mean the privation of religious rights, as religious rights are pivotal to human rights and human rights are pivotal to secularism—at least at the normative level. To me, secularism means that no religion should be allowed to impose its values on others against their will. It also means that the state should not favor any particular religion at the expense of another. Further, it means that taxpayers' money should not be used to promote a specific religion. I prefer to describe these values under the term secularity—in the institutional sense, removed from anti-religion ideological connotations.

Second, governments must refrain from interfering with religious groups and their institutions, except as required by law and in a manner that is fair and non-discriminatory. Whenever it is necessary to use public funds in a religiously oriented activity, such as supporting charitable activities through tax-exempt status or grants, it should be done in a fair and impartial manner.

How are we fairing on these issues in North America? Certainly there are several positive achievements. However, we need to be candid about the deficiencies, some of which are serious. Let me point them out in the form of several recommendations. Rather than pointing fingers, let's point to issues.

First, governments must refrain from supporting, encouraging, or funding, either directly or indirectly, current efforts to redefine Islam for Muslims, especially by recruiting and funding dissident elements who represent only a small minority of Muslims. This is somehow analogous to a Muslim government encouraging, recruiting, and funding a think tank to redefine Christianity for Christians, and then encouraging the dissemination of this information and shoving it down the throats of Christians. We should support free and open debates that pose honest and frank religious questions to other religious communities. However, we should reject hard-handed intervention. No group or government in any society should take it upon itself to act as the religious authorities of another religion or to choose such authorities for them. This attitude, which is bound to backfire sooner or later, is likely to be seen by others as a sinister attempt to create unnecessary division and discord in other religious communities.

Second, no religious group or institution should be singled out for harassment and scrutiny of the basis of prejudicial stereotypes and presumptions of guilt based on its members' association with or belonging to a certain ethnic or religious group. Nor should this be done on the basis of flimsy (and sometimes nonexistent) evidence, while hiding unfairly behind security and secrecy.

Third, it is everyone's duty to strive to repeal and/or modify some of the draconian provisions in the so-called U.S. Patriot Act, Canada's Bill 36, and similar undemocratic, potentially unconstitutional, and unpatriotic laws that were rushed through in the aftermath of the infamous 9/11 attack. Such laws, while appearing to be general, are tailor-made to victimize many American Muslims. In addition, they open the door for disproportionate profiling and the abuse of power against the Muslim community.

Finally, all individuals and institutions in society, especially religious groups, the media, and politicians, should not promote the voices of Islamophobia and other forms of religious and social bigotry. Rather, they should speak out against such voices with the same amount of repetition, clarity, and decisiveness that that they use to speak out against anti-Semitism. Anti-Islam is the same as anti-Semitism. Anti-Semitism includes Arab Semites and Jewish Semites. Both types of bigotry are immoral. They promote a culture of hate, which feeds the development of cultures of hate elsewhere. Both are dangerous.

THE EFFECTS OF POLICY

HUMAN RIGHTS VIOLATIONS FUEL ANTI-AMERICANISM
Chip Pitts

AFTER 9/11, THERE were many secret cases against Muslims in the United States on charges of terrorism, none of which resulted in convictions. Many Muslims were detained and deported. Many beatings and insults directed toward Islam occurred, and some people even died in custody. As documented by groups ranging from Amnesty International to CAIR, there was a rise in hate crimes and racism. All of this is discrimination, and it depends on stereotypes that are reinforced in media outlets, including Fox News and Sinclair Broadcasting. Pat Robertson says that Islam is a satanic religion. Anne Coulter says that we should invade Muslim countries, kill their leaders, and convert their people to Christianity. And so-called experts, such as Daniel Pipes, suggest that Muslims are terrorists, as if one out of every five people in the world could possibly be a terrorist. Such demagogic propaganda depends on ignorance.

Unfortunately, most Americans are too distracted by economic and other pressures these days to stay informed and correct their ignorance about Muslims. Many think that all Muslims are Arabs, when we know that only a minority are. Islam is as ethnically and culturally diverse as the world itself. Many people think that all Arabs are Muslims. They think that Islam is more violent than Christianity, when history teaches us that Christians started the Crusades. They think that Islam is an inherently intolerant religion, when history reveals that Jewish and Christian communities under Muslim rule were granted more rights than minorities in other civilizations. They think that Islam inherently subordinates women, when history teaches that the subordination of women has many sources. They think that Muslims are alienated from human rights. Of course human rights and social justice are just as much a part of Islam as they are of Christianity and Judaism.

There is no excuse for this sort of ignorance. But I have found that even scholars and Muslims themselves may not be aware that Muslim countries and diplomats were integrally involved in the creation of the Universal Declaration of Human Rights in 1948. Muslim countries joined the international community in this assertion of universal human rights, and Muslim women in particular played a vital role in guaranteeing women's rand family rights. The Qur'an has verses against the compulsion of belief and for religious freedom. These verses influenced all Muslim delegates at the United Nations when this document was being composed. All Muslim nations accepted the declaration, except Saudi Arabia, which abstained on two articles: the right to marry and the right to change religious belief. Since that time, Saudi Arabia has repeatedly accepted the declaration, at least in theory. We know that, both in practice and in reality, these rights are not universally respected by Muslim or non-Muslim nations.

Some people ask: "How compatible is Islam with democracy?" Yet people could have the same question right now about tendencies within the United States. The current American administration is using force to bring democracy to Iraq in a misguided adventure that has been accompanied by terrible torture and human rights abuses. Similar overbroad approaches are being used within the United States, threatening democracy at home. And this new American model is sadly being replicated around the world by various governments, including Britain, France, and Australia, that are now resorting to extended detention without meeting traditional standards of evidence. People may not know it, but the Patriot Act has been replicated worldwide. Many countries even have new anti-terror legislation modeled after some of its provisions. In addition, all the violations of the American Bill of Rights in the Patriot Act, including the abridgment of the freedom of speech, the freedom of religion, the freedom of expression, and the right to due process, are also violations of the Universal Declaration of Human Rights.

After 9/11, dictatorships and authoritarian regimes around the world stepped up their violation of human rights. We know that former Defense Secretary Donald Rumsfeld signed specific orders that allowed torture—in violation of the Geneva Conventions and international law. The president's lawyer Alberto Gonzales and other administration lawyers wrote now-infamous memos authorizing the use of torture. They have tried to redefine torture to suggest that anything short of death or serious organ failure is not torture. The United States has engaged in "extraordinary rendition" by sending people to countries like Egypt, Jordan, Morocco, and Uzbekistan—basically kidnapping people off the street to send them to these jurisdictions for coercive interrogation. In Uzbekistan, their idea of torture includes boiling people alive. Incredibly, these forms of torture are happening in the world with America's acquiescence. There has to be accountability and an end to impunity.

We know what is happening at Guantánamo Bay: religious insults; putting fake menstrual blood on someone's face, exposing detainees to women's breasts; and having the Qur'an stomped on, kicked, and placed in toilets. This is why we are seeing protests in Pakistan and around the world, because news like this makes it appear, contrary to the Bush administration's rhetoric, that this is not so much a war on terror as it is a war on Islam.

There is a direct correlation between withdrawing human rights and bombings in such places as Russia, Indonesia, and Saudi Arabia. So the measures in the United States and elsewhere that curtail human rights, such as racial profiling and indefinite detention, are worse than ineffective: They are actively counterproductive. These rights are of immense practical value, for they represent the crystallization of the wisdom of civilizations over several millennia. Such things as freedom of speech and association and belief offer a safety valve for peaceful gathering and dissent, instead of violence. Privacy allows a space for autonomous belief and conscience commensurate with human dignity and development. Speedy and fair trials on evidence obtained free from coercion and torture also avoid any buildup of resentment and ensure that the guilty will be punished instead of the innocent. The rights to confront witnesses, be represented by counsel, and see the evidence against you do the same thing.

By contrast, overbroad and abusive measures divert law enforcement's focus and attention away from the guilty to the innocent. They divert resources in the same way and undermine the cooperative trust and dialogue upon which successful intelligence depends. They damage such fundamental American values as checks and balances and fan the flames of anti-Americanism, putting us all at greater risk. By the military's own admission, and affirmed by the International Red Cross and others, more than eighty to ninety percent of the detainees held at Abu Ghraib and Guantánamo Bay are not members of al-Qaidah but are random people innocent of terrorism who were rounded up, often by bounty hunters. So, any security that relies on repressing and violating human rights is false security.

Various European countries, such as Holland, Sweden, Switzerland, and France, have changed their opinions about an open and free society, and, in particular, their opinions about Muslims. There is a new xenophobia in Europe, as well as an anti-Muslim feeling that was not there before. Islamophobia is also on the rise in the United States. The Real ID Act attempts to create a form of national identity card. People will be sent back to their country of origin because of this law; some seeking asylum will be sent back to their counties and will lose their lives. This is a sad departure from our nation's founding as a nation of immigrants who were often fleeing such religious and political persecution.

Non-Muslims and Muslims need to reach out to one another to challenge ignorance. Alternative media is a good resource to counter mainstream media. Communication and coalitions must happen. One might consider joining Amnesty International and encourage even greater attention to these issues.

According to the Qur'an:

> "O You who have attained to faith, be ever steadfast in your devotion to God, bearing witness to the truth in all equality, and never let hatred of anyone lead you into the sin of deviating from justice. Be just, [for] this is closest to being God-conscious. And remain conscious of God. Verily, God is aware of all you do." [31]

These are core values of the Universal Declaration of Human Rights and of Islam. We must protect the rights of Muslims and non-Muslims and see our interconnectedness with all people. We are all creatures of God with human dignity. Eleanor Roosevelt once posed the question "Where after all do universal human rights begin?" His answer: "In small places, closes to home—so close and so small that they cannot be seen on any map of the world. Yet they *are* the world of the individual person: The neighborhood he lives in; the school or college he attends;

the factory, farm or office where he works. Such are the places where every man, woman, and child seeks equal justice, equal opportunity, equal dignity without discrimination. Unless these rights have meaning there, they have little meaning anywhere. Without concerted citizen action to uphold them close to home, we shall look in vain for progress in the larger world."[32]

One can accomplish this by such little things as writing a letter to the editor of a town's newspaper, hosting a dinner in home, organizing an educational forum, or attending a city council meeting. Jody Williams is an example of one person who made a huge difference. Starting just with herself and an Internet connection, she won the Nobel Prize in 1997 for organizing, including a global e-mail campaign around the world, to ban the use of landmines.

In closing, I would like to share one of the most profound quotes I know. It is from Lutheran Pastor Martin Niemöller and exists in different versions. However, the following is one you hear often:

> "At first they came for the communists and I did not speak out because
> I was not a communist. Then they came for the socialists and I did not
> speak out because I was not a socialist. Then they came for the trade
> unionists and I did not speak out because I was not a trade unionist.
> Then they came for the Jews and I did not speak out because I was not
> a Jew. Then they came for me and there was no one left to speak out
> for me." [33]

We should not let this be said of Muslims—that we were silent in the face of injustice. We should speak up—and act.

American Imperialism Feeds Anti-Americanism

Louis Cantori

NTI-AMERICANISM AMONG MULSLIMS in the world, like its political extreme of terrorism, originates as a reaction to American foreign policy. It does not originate in the deep reservoirs of evil, hatred, and irrationality attributed to it by American policymakers. In other words, anti-Americanism is a rational phenomenon that can be explained by reason. In addition, while anti-Americanism originates as a foreign attitude directed against the American government, in fact its rationale is such that much of its content is shared by informed critics of American policy, non-Muslim and Muslim alike, foreign or domestic.

Anti-Americanism, to the extent to which each of us is a critic of American policy, is a charge against us. Anti-Americanism is something that, when looked at objectively, one sees a significant basis for why it exists. Having said the preceding, it is true there are two intellectual levels of anti-Americanism and criticism of American policy. The first, the most broad and volatile, consists of a reaction to what might be called the most general features of American policy. These broad features originate in what William Kristol, editor of the neoconservative *The Weekly Standard* and who was the director of the Project for a New American Century (PNAC), refers to as *Pax Americana*, the neoconservative version of American imperialism.

Let's be clear about this word *imperialism*, for it is an operative concept of neoconservatism. I was present in 2004 at a meeting involving two members of the Coalition Provisional Authority who had just come back from a meeting in Baghdad and were reporting to a group of fifty American civil servants in Washington, D.C. Each one of them began their remarks with a statement about the exhilaration and pleasure they were having in Baghdad in bearing the burdens of American imperialism. They said that American imperialism was a great and difficult burden, but that its pursuit was its own reward. Only one of then had the good grace to blush. I was personally, by the way, very angry with this. I could not believe what I was hearing. But I know where it started.

It started on this website: http://www.newamericancentury.org, which is the ideological center of the neoconservative movement. At its founding in 1997, it said that the objectives of the Project for a New American Century were to shape the new century, to further American democratic principles and American national interests simultaneously. This line of thought was later expanded in September 2000, in a neo-conservative defense-planning document called "Rebuilding American Defenses," signed by twenty-four prominent neoconservatives, including Paul Wolfowitz and William Kristoll.[34] They were detailing, before the 2000 election, three years before the war itself, and before the 9/11 attack, what was to be the war and invasion of Iraq. In other words, the war was premeditated and preplanned. Their stated objectives in this document are to preserve and extend this American peace or *Pax Americana*. They use the Latin term *pax*, as in *Pax Britannia, Pax Romana*, and *Pax Americana*.

These are three historical instances of imperialism. I want to focus on the normalcy of this word because otherwise we are inclined to think, like I did when I heard it said in this meeting, that this was leftist commentary or something extremely controversial. But this is not controversial to the neoconservatives. To some extent, this is what their foreign policies are really all about. In this process, democracy will become the means of all extending American interests.

As of this moment, American policy is engaged in rhetoric about the desirability of democracy in the Muslim world. At the same time, American policymakers are reluctant or refuse to engage Muslim organizations in the Middle East, and elsewhere in the world, in dialogue. I think the only prospect for cooperation and dialogue is if American Muslims take the initiative and begin to do this informally and among themselves, because if one waits for American policymakers to do it, it will not happen. We already know that Muslims have arrived politically. So, we are really in an absurd situation. For all practical purposes, Muslims are now in charge in the Middle East in all kinds of ways. Not literally, but they are at the door and ready to come through the door. We can talk about *al-Ikhwan al-Muslimun* (the Muslim Brotherhood) as a broad international organization. American Muslims have to talk to people in the region and create a practical situation in which American policymakers cannot ignore the initiatives that Americans would take.

In a recent conference, a senior American official was asked this very question. He wanted to say that our minds are open, but the only reply he could give was to look at the case of Turkey. In other words, what he was saying was give Mubarak fifty more years to beat the heads of the Muslims in Egypt, and fifty years from now, when Muslims organizations have been reduced organizationally and conditioned to behave politically in a certain way, the American government will open up communications with them. This was the logic of his reply.

Therefore, there are two main factors against which Muslims are reacting. The first, in the words of the American president, is that America is on a democratic ideological crusade to promote democracy among the peoples of the Middle East, the region that America wants to penetrate for security and energy reasons. The vision of an American crusade has resulted in what has become, to some critics, a sophisticated critique of liberal democracy as the crusade's message. In other words, the phrase *liberal democracy* has become the language of American imperialism. That is why we all have some ambivalence about the official American program for advocating democracy, because we sense what I have just said. This is a democracy that is being used for ulterior purposes. It is not what it appears to be, and this creates an incredible dilemma. Add to this the symbolism of the torture, abject humiliations, and religious insults that have occurred at Guantánamo Bay and Abu Ghraib.

There is also an even deeper basis of anti-Americanism, aside from these issues that I have just raised: a critique of the internal machinations during the formation of American-Iraqi policy and its relation to Israel. This begins with another website that one can visit to determine the accuracy of my narrative. The document, *A Clean Break*, was written in 1996 by Richard Perle and Douglass Feith, two of the major architects of the Iraq war,[35] as a planning document for then Israeli Prime Minister Benjamin Netanyahu. The day after they wrote it, Netanyahu made a speech before a joint session of the American Congress, during which he used some of its language. *A Clean Break* called for overthrowing Saddam Hussein in order to serve Israel's security interests.

All of the neoconservatives mentioned above were the ones who hatched the invasion of Iraq prior to 9/11. The later event was to be the convenient excuse for a premeditated war. In other words, the public's increasing knowledge of this document's content has forged an agreement between mass Muslim anti-Americanism, based on the broad themes of an American crusade and the offenses and humiliations against Islam, and a more sophisticated understanding that not only is the United States complicit in the occupation of Palestine, but that even the invasion of a Muslim country was intended to benefit Israel.

Therefore, one might conclude that while Muslims might be opposed to terrorism—which I think virtually all of them are—it becomes more difficult to separate oneself from the validity of Muslim anti-Americanism. It is perhaps even more difficult because it is accompanied by an awareness of these things on the one hand and by being a loyal American citizen on the other. At this moment, as Alexis DeTocqueville had anticipated in his famous *Democracy and America*, written in the 1830s, America is in the grip of the tyranny of the majority, which prevents practically any voice of dissent.

Although American Muslims have a critical view of the issues about which I am writing, there is a void of silence. There is no media outlet to voice these sentiments, and practically no impressive organizational ability to deal with them. Those who are Muslim and scholars are in the same position that I myself, as a Middle East specialist, am in as well. We find that there is no audience for the very things about which I have just addressed. This is a very pessimistic conclusion. My intention was to define, as objectively as possible, the problem with which we are all living at present.

THE ROLE OF THE MEDIA

POPULAR MEDIA AND OPINION LEADERS ARE TO BLAME

Samer Shehata

ISLAMOPHOBIA IN PUBLIC OPINION

ATTITUDES TOWARD ARABS, Muslims, and Islam in the United States are troubling and have not been improving over the last few years. Although survey data about American attitudes toward Muslims and Islam before 9/11 is not as readily available, one could reasonably assume that there has been a significant increase in negative feelings toward these groups and religion since 9/11. According to the Pew Research Center for the People and the Press,[36] attitudes toward Islam have been holding relatively stable during the last three years, with about 33-36 percent of respondents saying they hold unfavorable attitudes toward Islam as compared with 38-40 percent saying they hold favorable attitudes.[37]

Other polling has produced slightly more troubling findings. According to *Washington Post*/ABC News polls, the percentage of Americans who hold unfavorable views of Islam has risen over the last three years. In the immediate aftermath of 9/11, 39 percent of those polled stated that they held unfavorable views. This figure dropped to a low of 24 percent by January 2002, but has been steadily increasing ever since. In a recent *Washington Post*/ABC News poll released in March 2006, 46 percent of Americans said they held unfavorable views.[38] Although the Pew and the *Washington Post*/ABC News polling data differs to some extent, we can say with confidence that around 40 percent of Americans have negative or unfavorable views of Islam.

There is less variation in the polling data regarding American opinion about Islam and violence. A high percentage of Americans believe that Islam, more than other religions, encourages violence. The Pew surveys, for example, indicate that the percentage of Americans who believe that Islam is more likely to encourage violence, as compared to other religions, has increased from 25 percent in March 2002 to 36 percent in July 2005. The latter figure is below the high mark of 46 percent in July 2004.[39] A CBS News poll released at the end of February 2006 produced similar findings: 39 percent of respondents believed that Islam encourages violence, as compared to other religions.[40] The *Washington Post*/ABC News polls also found that the number of Americans who believe that Islam encourages violence against non-Muslims has increased significantly over the last three years, from 14 percent in January 2002 to 32 percent as of March 2006.[41]

A recent *Washington Post*/ABC News survey asked Americans about prejudice toward Muslims and Arabs. The poll asked the following question: "If you honestly assessed yourself, would you say that you have at least some feelings of prejudice against Muslims, or not?" The same question was asked about Arabs. About one-fourth of the respondents admitted to feelings of prejudice; 27 percent said they held prejudiced feelings against Muslims, whereas 25 percent said they had prejudiced feelings against Arabs.[42] The poll also asked the following, possibly even more revealing, question: "Have you recently heard other people say prejudiced things against Muslims, or not?" A little more than a third (34 percent) of respondents said yes, and a higher percentage (43 percent) reported recently hearing prejudiced things against Arabs.

An alarming number of Americans are quite willing to impose

extra security measures on Muslim and Arab Americans (e.g., carrying an extra form of government-issued identification or increased security requirements at airports). Many Americans also favor restricting immigration from Arab and Muslim countries. This trend began immediately after 9/11.

For example, after stating that there has been a "sharp shift toward increased wariness of Islam in post-9/11 America" and noting that "the proportion of the public calling Islamic fundamentalism a critical threat to vital U.S. interests has jumped 23 points to 61 percent," the Chicago Council on Foreign Relation's *Worldviews 2002* (June 2002) report notes that "Suspicion and concern extends to Arabs and Muslim peoples. By more than a three-to-one margin (76 percent to 22 percent), Americans say that based on the events of 9/11, U.S. immigration laws should be tightened to restrict the number of immigrants from Arab or Muslim countries into the United States, and 77 percent say that in order to combat terrorism they favor restricting overall immigration into the United States. A small majority, 54 percent to 43 percent, also favor using racial profiling in airport security checks in order to combat international terrorism."[43]

Unfortunately, it is not clear that such feelings have changed considerably in the years since 9/11. A *USA Today*/Gallup Poll conducted in the summer of 2005, for example, found that 53 percent of respondents favored "requiring all Arabs, including those who are U.S. citizens, to undergo special, more intensive security checks before boarding airplanes in the US," and 46 percent favored "requiring Arabs, including those who are U.S. citizens, to carry a special ID." The good news is that 53 percent were opposed to the idea of requiring Arabs to carry special IDs. This, however, should not be considered comforting, as any significant percentage of the American public holding such views should be disturbing.[44]

All of the polling data confirms that Americans, by self-admission, do not know very much about Islam, its teachings, or principles despite the fact that there has been a tremendous amount of coverage about the Middle East and Islam in all of the various American media outlets over the last several years.[45] According to the Pew surveys, for example, only 51 percent of those polled were able to identify the Qur'an as the Muslims' holy book (the Islamic equivalent of the Bible) and only 48 percent "correctly identified Allah as the name Muslims use to refer to God." An absolute majority of Americans (66 percent), the poll found, said they know "nothing at all" or "not very much" about Islam.[46]

The *Washington Post*/ABC News poll asked the question in a slightly different manner but produced very similar results. The poll asked Americans "Do you feel you do or do not have a good basic understanding of the teachings and beliefs of Islam, the Muslim religion?" Nearly 60 percent of respondents answered "no," while 40 percent answered "yes." What is possibly most fascinating in all of the polling data is the correlation between American's views toward Islam and a number of other factors. Both the Pew and the *Washington Post*/ABC News polls establish a relationship between four variables and Americans' attitudes toward Islam: 1) knowledge of the religion, 2) one's own religion, 3) political views, and 4) age.

The good news is that existing polling data establish a positive relationship between both one's knowledge of Islam and one's educational attainment and attitudes toward it. Those who are more knowledgeable about Islam are more likely to view it favorably. Similarly, educational attainment is positively correlated with favorable opinions of Islam. Fifty-three percent of those with a four-year college degree had a favorable opinion, as compared to only 28 percent of those who had only a high school education or less.[47]

What is possibly most intriguing, however, is that both polls established a relationship between the religion of those polled and their views toward Islam, with white evangelical Protestants more likely to have unfavorable views of Islam (including prejudiced thoughts) than other religious groups or "secularists." According to the *Washington Post*/ABC News poll: "While 46 percent of all Americans have an unfavorable opinion of Islam overall, among evangelical white Protestants it's 61 percent. Likewise, evangelical white Protestants are 12 points more apt to think Islam encourages violence and nine points more apt to say it teaches intolerance. And 36 percent of evangelical white Protestants admit to some feelings of prejudice against Muslims" (compared to 27 percent of the general population).[48]

The Pew poll produced similar findings and added that, "Among religious groups, favorable attitudes toward Muslim-Americans are most prevalent among white Catholics (61 percent)."[49] Both polls also established that Republicans are more likely to hold negative views of Islam than Democrats. The Pew poll determined that only 33 percent of conservative Republicans held favorable views of Islam, compared to 56 percent of liberal Democrats—a 25 percent difference.[50] The Pew poll also established a relationship between political conservatism and the likelihood of holding negative or unfavorable views of Islam. For example, moderate/liberal Republicans were more favorable than conservative Republicans, whereas conservative/moderate Democrats were less favorable than their liberal counterparts. Both polls also determined a relationship between age (or generation) and views toward Islam, with younger Americans tending to have more positive views and those 65 years or older more likely to hold negative views.[51]

News, Popular Culture, and Public Discourse

The next logical question is what is behind these figures? Why do many Americans hold negative views of Islam, believe that Islam is more likely than other religions to encourage violence, and hold prejudicial feelings against Arabs and Muslims? Part of the answer, of course, has already been established by the data itself: ignorance. Americans know very little about Islam, and the more they know about it, along with increased familiarity with Muslims and Arabs (e.g., as neighbors, work colleagues or classmates) in addition to higher levels of education, the less likely they are to hold negative views of Islam or of Muslims and Arabs. In other words, like other forms of bigotry and racism, ignorance and unfamiliarity are primary culprits.

A related question is if Americans do not know very much about Islam, then where do they get the little "information" (or "knowledge") they do have about it and about Muslims and Arabs?[52] The media is likely to be one of the answers to this question. Television news and popular culture are surely among the primary sources of "information" and exposure to Islam, Muslims, and Arabs for many Americans. Of course, the media are quite heterogeneous and include everything from serious print newspapers and journals to tabloids, PBS documentaries to afternoon talk radio and mass popular culture. Let me limit my discussion to only two media forms: television news and television popular culture.

One could argue that news, particularly television news, is inherently biased against all good news, including news that would depict Arabs, Islam, and Muslims in a generally more positive light. As the old saw has it: "If it bleeds, it leads." Violence, killing, conflict, and hatred (generally bad stuff) always takes precedence over "good news," whether we are discussing news about suburban Washington, DC, or world events. The important point here is that news is *universally biased against good news*, not simply or only biased against Islam, Arabs, or Muslims.[53]

What this means for residents of Washington, DC, for example, is that local news is dominated by stories of drive-by shootings, student deaths at troubled area highs schools, and other crime-and violence-related topics. What this means for coverage of the Middle East and the Muslim world in the United States is that the news is dominated by the Iraq war, Osama bin Laden, terrorism, and beheadings. This type of bad or negative news dominates coverage, and Islam, in the process, becomes synonymous with jihad. And jihad, of course, is understood in a particular way: as irrational, unjustified, religiously based violence (usually against non-Muslims). There are far fewer stories in the American news about Ramadan, for example, or Islam and ethical values, the Organization of the Islamic Conference, or ordinary Muslim Americans.

My own experience with the media reflects this. Although I am frequently called upon by the American media (e.g., television, radio, and print journalists) to discuss the Middle East and the Arab world, out of the hundreds, if not the thousands, of times I have been called for interviews, I can only recall two stories that were positive: a CNN story about Shirin Ibadi, the Iranian lawyer and human rights activist, receiving the Nobel Prize, and an article about tourism in Libya for an obscure travel magazine. In comparison, I have done several thousand interviews about al-Qaidah, terrorist attacks in Saudi Arabia, the ongoing Palestinian-Israeli conflict, and similar topics.

The point is that when the Middle East, Arabs, and Muslims make it into the news, it is usually in the context of negative (or unfavorable) events. In the process, the kinds of things Americans hear about Islam, Muslims, and Arabs are more often negative and unpleasant.

When discussing representations of Arabs and Muslims in the United States, we cannot neglect or underestimate the importance of popular culture. Portrayals of Arabs and Muslims in popular culture exhibit even worse tendencies than those found in the news media. Many Americans spend more time watching television serials than news, serious documentaries, or educational programs. Popular culture is also not constrained by the potentially mitigating effects of the need to be "balanced," "objective," or "professional" like the news media.

Well before 9/11, Arabs and Muslims were frequently depicted as terrorists and religious fanatics in American popular culture. This has long been demonstrated by such works as Jack Shaheen's The TV Arab (Bowling Green State University Popular Press: 1984) and Reel Bad Arabs (Interlink Publishing Group: 2001) or Melani McAlister's Epic Encounters: Culture, Media, and US Interests in the Middle East, 1945-2000 (University of California Press: 2001) or Edward Said's classic

Covering Islam (Pantheon: 1981). The situation has worsened considerably in the last few years, however.

It is quite remarkable, in fact, what has happened to American popular culture since 9/11. There has been a tremendous increase in television serials about terrorism, counter-terrorism, the CIA, and similar agencies on all networks (e.g., "The Agency," "The Grid," "Alias," "24," "Threat Matrix," and a new show entitled "DHS, Department of Homeland Security").[54] There is even a show called "Sleeper Cell," about "an undercover FBI agent who is seduced into joining an Islamic sleeper terrorist cell in the United States."[55] Moreover, existing shows quickly incorporated similar themes in their programs after 9/11 (e.g., "The West Wing" and "The Practice").

Although a small number of these programs deal with some of these issues more intelligently than others and from a number of perspectives (e.g., "The Practice" featured a program about discrimination against Arab Americans, for example), the majority reproduce the standard stereotypes of Arabs and Muslims as terrorists who are fanatically committed to killing innocents.[56]

Arguably the most popular of these shows is Fox Television's smash hit "24," which is now available in the Middle East thanks to Dubai's One Television Network. The third season featured the following plot: An ordinary Muslim family in the United States is, in fact, a sleeper cell. The family orchestrates an elaborate plot to melt down a number of nuclear reactors throughout the country, kill the president, and detonate a nuclear weapon in a large American city. In the course of the show, they manage to shoot down Air Force One, injure the president, and steal nuclear missiles. The show does include a few "good Muslims" playing minor roles, a disclaimer at the beginning of the season reassuring viewers that "the American Muslim community stands firmly beside their fellow Americans in denouncing and resisting all forms of terrorism," and a plot twist in the end that ties the Chinese to terrorism.

But the negative stereotypes and images of Muslims and Islam are recurring. "24" and other shows go even further, however, suggesting to Americans that the Muslim family next door could be a sleeper cell committed to inflicting mass casualties against its fellow citizens. We must ask: Would it be appropriate if the "bad guys" in these shows were consistently Protestant, Catholic, or Jewish?

It would be easy to blame American popular culture for much of the negative feelings and prejudice toward Arabs, Muslims, and Islam. And some amount of blame is certainly well-deserved. But we must also ask ourselves if these shows produce stereotypes and negative images, or do they simply articulate and reproduce already existing sentiments, fears, anxieties, and ignorance? Are they the proverbial chicken or the egg, or are they something in between?

OPINION LEADERS

Surely another factor involved in the negative views of Americans toward Arabs, Muslims, and Islam is what some prominent Americans say about Islam. Pollsters call these people "opinion leaders" because their statements and writings leave an impact on wider public views. Although President Bush has made positive statements about Islam on several occasions (and has been criticized for this as well), a number of prominent Americans (and non-Americans[57]) have said dreadful things about the religion. For example, Jerry Falwell, an influential Baptist minister and founder of the Moral Majority, said on the popular American news show "60 Minutes": "I think Muhammad was a terrorist. ... Jesus set the example for love, as did Moses, and I think Muhammad set an opposite example."[58] Reverend Franklin Graham, Billy Graham's son, has repeatedly called Islam an "evil" religion that preaches violence. Pat Robertson, the founder of the Christian Coalition, has described Muhammad as an "absolute wild-eyed fanatic…a robber and brigand … a killer."[59]

At least one high-ranking American government official has made negative statements about Islam. Lt. General William Boykin, the undersecretary of defense for intelligence, said this when describing his battle with a Somali (Muslim) warlord: "I knew that my God was bigger than his God. I knew that my god was a real God and his was an idol." Boykin has also said that America's enemy in the "war on terrorism" is "a spiritual enemy … called Satan," and that "radical Muslims" hate the United States "because we're a Christian nation, because our foundation and roots are Judeo-Christian and the enemy is a guy named Satan.":[60]

These are only some of the best-known examples of anti-Islamic discourse in the United States. There are countless others, especially on the extreme right, such as Ann Coulter, Rush Limbaugh, Sean Hannity, and Daniel Pipes, all of whom regularly make bigoted anti-Islamic remarks. In March 2006, for example, Pipes wrote an article, "Sudden Jihad Syndrome," in which he discussed the possibility of regular, ordinary Muslims becoming homicidal: "This is what I have dubbed the Sudden Jihad Syndrome, whereby normal-appearing Muslims abruptly become violent. It has the awful but legitimate consequence of casting suspicion on all Muslims. Who knows whence the next jihadi? How can one be confident a law-abiding Muslim will not suddenly erupt in a homicidal rage?"

The ranting of Falwell and Pipes are only the most obvious and vulgar forms of anti-Islamic bigotry in the United States today.

There is also a more subtle and sophisticated (and therefore more respectable) anti-Islamic discourse in the US. We can call this the "Islam as Problem" discourse. Its proponents say that Islam is an obstacle to democracy, uncomfortable with or incapable of being modern, oppresses women, and encourages violence and terrorism (e.g., jihad and martyrdom). A number of prominent writers and intellectuals have said as much., Bernard Lewis writes about "Islam" as a civilization long since in decline.[63] Samuel Huntington claims that Islam is unconducive to democracy (in addition to his more famous "clash of civilizations" thesis), while Francis Fukayama describes radical Islamists as the fascists of the modern world. Thomas Friedman writes about Islam and modernity in a way tha t implies that we (Westerns) are modern while Muslims are not.[64]

In this discourse, the problem is "Islam" itself, not particular extremists and their specific *interpretations* of Islam in the political, social, and historical contexts in which they find themselves. All of the ills of the so-called Muslim world are a direct result of Islam, taken as a self-evident category, an unchanging essence, outside of history, across space and time, and independent of real living Muslims (people).

Understandably, the last few years have been difficult for Arabs and Muslims in the United States. Even if one has not been subjected to discrimination, prejudice, or hate crimes since 9/11 (and there has been a marked increase in the number of hate crimes against Arabs and Muslims, or those perceived to be Arabs or Muslims, such as Sikhs and South Asians, in the United States), the general environment has become less welcoming and more threatening.[65] In addition to the Patriot Act, the Iraq war, the Abu Ghraib prison scandal, and other events, many Arab and Muslim Americans feel under siege and psychologically and emotionally exhausted as a result of the constant bombardment of anti-Arab and Anti-Muslim discourse.

AL-JAZEERA IS NOT THE CULPRIT
Hafiz al-Mirazi

ISLAMOPHOBIA IS AN illegal, irrational reaction and a psychological problem. Such a claim really takes the blame off of those people who discriminate against Islam or Muslims. If we reduce this problem to a phobia, someone will be exonerated in a court of law. If we use the terms *anti-Americanism* or *anti-Semitism*, we should also speak of Islamophobia as *anti-Islam*.

People are speaking against the faith. Muslim leaders are not allowed to participate in certain political meetings because of the rhetoric against Islam, yet such people as Franklin Graham are allowed to lead prayers in the White House and during the president's inauguration. Rhetoric against Islam, from other groups and from such people as Franklin Graham, has its roots in anti-Islamic and anti-Muslim feelings, which manifest themselves as hate crimes. According to CAIR, such hate crimes rose by 50 percent after 9/11. I would attribute this to a rise in awareness concerning the rights of American Muslims, rather than to an actual increase in incidents. People in the past did not report these crimes because they did not want to be harassed or go to jail.

If people have a phobia, they can repress or contain their feelings. We see a successful campaign to support the rights of our Jewish brothers and sisters and to combat anti-Semitism. It does not mean that all Americans have positive feelings toward all Jews–or toward all Hindus, for that matter. It simply means that this society does not accept anti-Semitism and that people will pay a price for this kind of discrimination. One can feel whatever he/she wants about other people, just as long as he/she does not step on their rights or hurt their feelings. Human rights should be protected.

Al-Jazeera deals with anti-Americanism directly. But it is not about anti-national origin or feelings against a country. Sometimes a country is reduced to a government. For example, some people express feelings that can be labeled anti-Bush, anti-Bush administration, or anti-Republican. When people in the West, such as in Washington, DC, and London, protest against the Bush administration, they are not called anti-American. Yet similar protests in the Arab world are labeled as being anti-American. When these protests happen in Egypt, Jordan, and elsewhere in the Muslim world, Western media outlets report them as anti-American demonstrations.

One wonders why the same anti-war slogans and goals are labeled as being anti-American when they appear in some societies, but are somehow not anti-American when they appear in other societies. Things are simplified. They try to link the ruler with the state. People assume that protests against the ruler are protests against the state.

This is what we face with media coverage: mixing patriotism with journalism. Any questioning of the government's acts is considered an act of disloyalty to the country. Al-Jazeera has been accused of being anti-Saudi, anti-Moroccan, anti-Jordanian, anti-Egyptian, and so on. Not all criticism against a government is criticism against the entire country. If one criticizes Mubarak, is one criticizing Egypt? If one criticizes Bush, is one criticizing the United States? People should be able to distinguish criticism against a ruler or an administration from criticism against an entire nation.

Once, al-Jazeera tried to find out why the Pentagon wanted to establish the Office of Strategic Influence. This was a government outlet using taxpayer dollars to disseminate misinformation and lies to the international media in order to counter what government officials were calling anti-Americanism. Thank God, according to the *New York Times* and the *Washington Post*, these efforts have been stopped.

The government was also thinking of establishing government-run media outlets for the Arab world, such as al-Hura Television and Radio Sawa. A reporter at a major network, trying to find an excuse for the Bush administration, suggested that the administration had to do this in order to counter the Arab media and their anti-American questioning. This reporter used some of the videos that I had given him out of courtesy for an interview that I had conducted with Secretary Powell in April 2005. His network displayed my face, without any audio, and said that this was a representation of anti-American questioning from the Arab media. Then it included a sound bite from Powell questioning me. Secretary Powell said: "Well, I would not agree with the way you put your question, but I would say…" Nobody knew what the question was that he did not agree with or what kind of anti-Americanism I was being accused of in my question.

This is a fellow, in what is supposed to be a respectable media outlet, with two violations. According to the copyrights and the rules of fair use, the footage we gave him was supposed to be used within forty-eight hours. Instead, he used it a month later without any credit or payment and, moreover, distorted the actual question. The question was something about applying the same rules to Israel as the United States does to the Arab world. It was much less critical than Powell would have faced in the American media. After seeing the actual video, someone in the Arab media accused me of being too polite. He said that the American official had given us propaganda and nonsense, and that I had allowed him to say whatever he had wanted to say. This is an example of being labeled as anti-American for questioning the government's policies or statements.

Another example is evident in some of the reactions and counter-reactions to the abhorrent acts of disrespect directed toward the Qur'an at the Guantánamo Bay detention center. When protests erupted in Pakistan and Afghanistan because of these actions, the *Washington Post* and *New York Times* reported that these were anti-American protests. The issue here is not anti-Americanism. People are against an action that the White House, the State Department, and the Pentagon all had said, that if true, was not acceptable and that people would be punished. So if we agree that this act is not acceptable, why do we label those who protest it as being anti-American?

Anyway, the source of the Guantánamo controversy, which led to the "anti-American sentiment" in the Arab and Muslim world, was *Newsweek*, not Al-Jazeera. Was anti-American *Newsweek* printing this propaganda, or were our people reacting to real events and issues that were being reported, whether they were true or not? Look at the Abu Ghraib scandal, the whole distortion, and the negative image of the United States abroad— not just in the Arab world, but throughout the civilized world. CBS put the story out, not an Arab or a Muslim media outlet.

So instead of facing the issue, some try to scapegoat the media, sometimes the Arab media and even the American media. There are a lot of problems in the Muslim world, and Muslims should not always blame the American media for distorting their image. Instead, they should work more on improving the reality on the ground, both in the Muslim world and in the United States.

THE PROBLEM IS KNEE-JERK REACTIONS AND COUNTER-REACTIONS

Claude Salhani

WHAT EXACTLY IS Islamophobia? In truth, I was not quite sure of the real meaning, other than that it is the combination of two words: *Islam* and the Greek word *phobos*. The latter meaning denotes an exaggerated, usually inexplicable and illogical, fear of a particular class, object, or situation. Note that the definition includes the word *inexplicable*. *Phobia*, in short, means that we fear something, yet we do not really know what we fear or why we fear it. However, that fear is nevertheless there–and it is real. Many of those who fear Islam do not really know why they fear it. Their fear is inexplicable and, furthermore, illogical.

So looking to find out more about what Islamophobia means, I do what I do as a journalist when I am not really sure what a word means: I went to my dictionary and looked it up. Webster's did not have a definition of Islamophobia. So I looked at the publishing date. It was the tenth edition, printed in 1993.

Much has changed in fourteen years. To begin with, we have lived through the terrible 9/11 tragedy. The wars in Afghanistan and Iraq have done a lot to change relations between Islamic countries, Muslims in general, and the United States. I then consulted Webster's on-line dictionary and still got nothing. Ultimately, after some research, the only definition I could find was just three short words: prejudice against Muslims. Now one must admit that this does not shed much light on the matter. But it is, I found, rather appropriate. Most people who are prejudiced against Islam or Muslims, or against any other religion or race for that matter, are simply ignorant and do not understand the real issues. It is easy to say we are anti-this or anti-that, or that we do not like Muslims or someone else. But when you ask for a detailed explanation, you find that they have a hard time coming up with one.

So where does this phobia come from? Regarding Islamophobia, I did some quick research that yielded some frightening results. A 2004 survey found that nearly half of the citizens in this nation believe that the United States government should restrict the civil liberties of all Muslim Americans. At the same time, most Americans remain ignorant of Islam, despite the fact that Islam is one of the fastest growing religions in the United States. Yet one in four Americans regard the Muslims living among them with suspicion. This suspicion, or rather this fear or phobia of Muslims, grew considerably in the aftermath of 9/11. I think that if one were to ask the average American prior to 9/11 about Muslims, they probably would not have had a second thought.

Now if we begin to look for a simple explanation of a very complicated and complex subject, I would venture to say that it might be because all nineteen hijackers turned out to be Muslims and Arabs. Added to this is the fact that there were mixed responses to the attacks from the Muslim world—mostly from the Arab world—which had a big role in building up animosity in the United States vis-à-vis the Muslim world. The fact that some people in the Palestinian territories, for example, danced in the streets at the news of the falling Twin Towers did not reflect well on Muslims as a whole. And many in the United States media did not bother, or did not know how, to make the distinction or to explain how such anger can rise to the surface.

What is it that makes these people so angry and so upset that they will rejoice at such horror? That, I think, is something the media was unable to explain properly. I generalize, of course, when I say "the media," but I think that this statement is, to a certain extent, true. Most Americans, unfortunately, of course immediately associated the attacks with Muslims in general. One has to say that some governments in the Islamic world did not help their cause. Had Saudi Arabia, for example, initially come out and denounced the attacks, rather than refuse to admit that the hijackers were from Saudi Arabia, it could have helped diffuse the situation. However, they had a hard time admitting to it.

Shortly after the attacks, I attended a meeting in Washington, DC, arranged by a Washington think tank. The organizers brought in some Saudi thinkers, professors, and doctors and said they were going to explain to us how 9/11 came about. My colleagues from the press and I went there expecting to hear an explanation; instead, they attacked us. They said that the American media was responsible for blowing it out of proportion. So, in a way it was natural for Americans to turn around and blame the Muslim world.

I am not excusing the knee-jerk reaction, but simply trying to explain something that is quite complicated. I would venture to say that if people from Nepal or Venezuela had attacked the United States, the reaction would have been the same toward Nepal or Venezuela. As it turns out, the attackers came from the Arab world. So naturally, the United States media was quick to pick up on the issue and began to analyze why they hate us— they, of course, being the Muslims.

It is important to remember that with the exception of a few journalists and a few specialists who know the topic (the Middle East and Islam), a good portion of the United States media is generally ignorant about Islam and its rich culture. Its members know little about what it stands for and thus cannot speak about Islam with any real authority. Reporters who normally cover state capitals and city halls found themselves propelled into one of the biggest stories of the decade, on a topic about which they knew very little, and often had to deal with people speaking in foreign languages that they did not understand. If anything, I believe there was more confusion than clarity in the post-9/11 days, weeks, months, and so on.

Here is a pertinent question to ask: Did the Bush administration make use of blurred lines to go after its enemies, at times its perceived enemies, and potential harmers of the state? I think there is little doubt that it made use of every advantage to do just that. Again, I am not condoning these actions, but rather am trying to offer an explanation.

Now I am a firm believer that not all blame comes from one side alone. Part of the problem, I believe, is that there was no unified voice speaking for Islam. And, more importantly, for moderate Muslims, who, after all, represent the majority of the world's 1.2 billion Muslims. Osama bin Laden and his followers were naturally given a great amount of ink and airtime in the American media and Islam was perceived as the enemy. At times, President Bush made attempts to demonstrate that Muslims are not the enemy, such as when he met with leaders of the Muslim community and tried to portray a different image. But he then turned around and chose words such as *crusade*, which put everything back to square one.

If the communication traffic flows in only one direction, there is no dialogue. Muslims, both individuals and organizations, must demonstrate a concerted effort to combat radicalism. Ill-aimed *fatwas* (religious opinions informed by knowledge of Islamic law) flying off the cuff should be stopped and refuted as being contrary to Islam.[66] Real efforts must be made to change what is still being taught in many schools in parts of southwest Asia and other parts of the world. As the saying goes, it is often the few rotten apples that spoil the bunch.

The way to help solve these issues is dialogue, not consistent threats of lawsuits, as, for example, CAIR has often done when it perceived real or imagined attacks against Islam, Muslims, or their organizations. The reality is that threatened lawsuits often only create greater animosity. A forced retraction, which one may get by using such a tactic, will get you words in the newspapers and on the air. However, it will only create greater schisms between the organizations concerned. At the end of the day, editors dislike being pushed around and bullied.

My personal belief is that a far better way is to write a politely addressed letter or send an invitation to discuss the issues over lunch. This will bring much more benefit in terms of public relations than threats, which journalists are sometimes used to and greatly dislike. Furthermore, personal contacts will help create a relationship between the organization and the media. When such a personal connection exists, one starts thinking to himself/herself: "I know that person. I met them. He/She is a human being. He/She relates to what I have to say—as opposed to an impersonal e-mail exchange or a formal letter from a lawyer."

In a free and democratic system such as the one that exists in the United States, groups are more likely to achieve their long-term objectives through education and persuasion. Threats, while they do command attention, do little if anything to resolve problems. Certainly, the American media needs to be better educated and must not generalize when it comes to Muslims. Muslims are not alone in making this quite legitimate complaint about the media. But I believe the educational process would be better served if an adversarial approach were avoided.

It is up to the leaders of the Islamic community to take concrete steps to erase this persistent phobia and get the message across in a friendly, non-adversarial manner. As the great Chinese thinker Sun Tzu said: "You need to see things as they are, not as you would like them to be."

THE ROLE OF
FAITH COMMUNITY LEADERS

What is Taking Place Is a Clash of Cousins

James Jones

GENERALLY, I DO not believe conspiracy theories. However, one only has to read the news, listen to talk radio and surf the internet a little bit to know that there is an on-going concentrated and coordinated attack on Muslims and Islam in this country. There is absolutely no question in my mind about this. It is clear that some people and groups openly encourage discrimination against Muslims and Islam in the United States. CAIR has responded by taking the strategic position that we Muslims are here and committed to having a role in this civil society and that we will not accept prejudice because of our religion. I think CAIR should be commended for their work. Yet we should recognize the distinction between malicious attacks and mistaken representations. In the relationships between members of faith communities it is latter that is more prevalent.

In approaching misconception of Christians and Muslims in public discourse, I offer three points:

- From the Muslim perspective, Jews, Christians and Muslims are spiritual and biological cousins.
- Negative categorizations of Muslims in the public discourse tend to fuel the idea of a "clash of civilizations."
- Christians and Muslims need to capitalize on our commonalities.

Unlike Dr. Samuel Huntington in his infamous book *Clash of Civilizations*, I would argue that much of the problem between Christians and Muslims (or the Western World and the Muslim World) is caused by the fact is that we are so similar—that is, we are cousins. In the Muslim narrative, we see ourselves as children of Abraham. We are biological and spiritual descendents of Abraham and Hagar (Hagjar) and Ishmael—their son. Biologically, we are children of Ishmael because we see him as the father of the Arabs, out of whom came Prophet Muhammad. The Christians are descendents of Abraham through Isaac. They claim their lineage through Moses, the Jews and ultimately Jesus Christ. I often remind my Christian audiences that Jesus was Jewish, a fact that is often obscured in Christian theology and practice. This *din* (religion) named Islam came from the same part of the world as the Abraham-linked faiths called Christianity and Judaism.

Spiritually, from the Muslim perspective, Abraham is the role model for the Prophet Muhammad, and a role model for all of humanity. This is clear in the Qur'an[67] and it is one of the things that Muslims agree upon when interpreting the Qur'an. Abraham as role model is something that Muslims and Christians have in common. In addition, Muslims and Christians share similar core values that support justice, fairness, and other universal ethical principles.

So, we are really looking at a "clash of cousins" rather than a clash of civilizations, because we lay claim to the same biological/geographical family and a very similar moral/ethical ethos. Consequently, Christians are taught to preach the justice-based message of Jesus Christ, and Muslims are taught to enjoin the right and forbid the wrong.[68] Nevertheless, we have frequently clashed physically (as we are reminded by the recent release of the new film about the Crusades, *The Kingdom of Heaven*). In spite of this difficult, often contentious history between Christians and Muslims, I would like to mention briefly one example of a peace-oriented moral competition that should be coming from this clash of cousins.

When I grew up in Virginia, I could get arrested, as a "colored" boy for drinking from the "white" fountain in a downtown Roanoke, Virginia store. This was in spite of the fact that both fountains were attached to the same pipe! Today, we have a similar illogical situation in Jerusalem where Palestinians are second-class citizens in the land of their birth. If racism and second class citizenship was wrong in Roanoke, Virginia in 1956, it is wrong in Israel/Palestine in 2007. If Christians, Muslims and Jews want to clash about something let in be in competing to see who can be the most just in a situation like this. This recommendation too conforms to the teachings of the Qur'an.[69]

My second point: Negative categorizations of Muslims in the public discourse tend to fuel the idea of a clash of civilizations. Consider the term "moderate Muslims." It is somewhat similar to terminology that comes out of the Sunni-Shia distinction in Islam. The term "Sunni Muslim" is redundant since most of us who call ourselves Muslims automatically assume that the word "Muslim" means that we follow the *Sunnah*, the authenticated traditions of Prophet Muhammad.

The larger point here is that such linguistic manipulation is an example of what I call *psycho-politics*. That is, language is being used in a way to support mental constructs that reinforce/advance a political idea and/or in order to maintain present power relationships. The only reason a Sunni calls himself or herself a Sunni is because of the existence of Shia. We are saying something like, "I just want to let you know I am not like those other people."

In the case of the term "moderate Muslims," what does it make me if I do not call myself a "moderate"? Does that automatically make me an extremist? I think forces from outside the Muslim community encourage and benefit from this type of "divide and conquer" psycho-political terminology. I have a similar issue with the term "Islamist".

Media pundits like Dr. Daniel Pipes makes Islamist sound like a dirty word. This is all psycho-politics. It can be seen as part of a larger struggle to persuade people to accept a particular point of view.

Such negative categorization of Muslims in the public discourse tends to marginalize and privatize all religious practice while fueling the "clash" theory. Islam is not the only religious group that has extremists. Karen Armstrong's discussion of religious extremism in her book, *The Battle for God* (Ballantine Books: 2001), makes this point quite persuasively. [70]

I concur with Professor William Schweiker when he argued that intellectuals need to diffuse the clash of civilizations idea by reigning in extremism from their co-religionists. He also pointed out that the cross-fertilization of ideas between civilizations has been going on for centuries.[71] For example, we wouldn't have modern medicine as we know it if cross-fertilization didn't occur between European Christian culture and European Muslim culture. In addition, Muslim intellectuals need to reign in the Muslim fanatics, and Christian intellectuals need to reign in Christian fanatics.

My third point is that Christians and Muslims need to capitalize on our commonalities. One way we can build Christian–Muslims relationships in America is to remember that Christianity and Islam both have large numbers of African Americans. With our common ethos and some common beliefs about Jesus Christ, African Americans and other former Christian Muslims can be useful in building bridges with the Christian community. However, in such a situation we need to remember that Muslims, Christians, and African American religious experiences all have sexist influences. Consequently, all of these groups still have some work to do when it comes to justice in the area of gender. Perhaps one common agenda that we Muslims and Christians can all apply ourselves to is rooting out sexism in our respective communities.

Marginalizing women is not healthy for either community. As Martin Luther King Jr. said, "We are caught in a web of mutuality. I cannot be what I aught to be, until you are what you aught to be."[72] Further, Malcolm X said, "I am for truth no matter who speaks it. I am for justice no matter who it is for or against. I am a human being first and foremost, and as such, I am for whatever benefits mankind as a whole."[73] Let us apply these ideals to the just treatment of women as a way for Christians and Muslims to capitalize on our commonalities.

In closing, I offer the following from the Qur'an, "O mankind! Be careful of your duty to your Lord Who created you from a single soul and from it created its mate and from them twain hath spread abroad a multitude of men and women."[74] Let us change the discourse between Christians, Muslims with this universal idea of common human family in mind.

WE SHOULD BUILD ON THE GREAT VALUES SHARED BY ALL RELIGIONS

Muzammil Siddiqi

ISLAMOPHOBIA AND ANTI-AMERICANISM have created a large gulf between our two cultures. Many people on both sides of the stream—not only Americans, but Muslims as well—now believe that we have nothing in common. This is the core of the problems of Islamophobia and anti-Americanism. I will focus on defining mainstream religious values that I believe are found in the various creed systems and possess the answer to prejudice.

It is the nature of extremism to hold that "we" are different from "them," and that "they" are different from "us." We are good and they are evil, and we must control them and hate them. This is how extremism emerges and grows and, eventually, leads to wars and violence. I do not accept this premise. We have many things in common that derive from our common sense, common humanity, concerns, issues, and problems. Generally, we find that human responses are very much the same, regardless of our religion or culture.

Furthermore, Christians, Jews, and Muslims have a common heritage. We share many things from our Abrahamic heritage. If one examines the 613 commandments of Orthodox Judaism, one can see how many are shared with other religious traditions. As a Muslim, I agree with many of these moral principles. I totally agree with the Ten Commandments and the Sermon on the Mount. So we have many things in common. The following table has every one of the Ten Commandments and the corresponding verses of the Qur'an:

Old Testament (Exodus)	Qur'an
20:3: Thou shalt have no other gods before me.	17:22: Do not associate another deity with God.
	47:19: Know therefore that there is no god but God.
20:4-6: Thou shalt not make unto thee any graven image, or any likeness of any thing that is in heaven above, or that is in the earth beneath, or that is in the water under the earth....	6:103: No visions can encompass Him, but He encompasses all visions.
	14:35: My Lord, make this a peaceful land, and protect me and my children from worshiping idols.
	42:11: There is nothing that equals (like) Him.
20:7: Thou shalt not take the name of the Lord thy God in vain; for the Lord will not hold him guiltless that taketh his name in vain.	2:224: Do not use God's name in your oaths as an excuse to prevent you from dealing justly.
	73:8: Remember the name of your Lord and devote yourself to Him exclusively.
	76:25: Glorify the name of your Lord morning and evening.
20:8-11: Remember the sabbath day, to keep it holy. Six days shalt thou labour, and do all thy work: But the seventh day is the sabbath of the Lord thy God: in it thou shalt not do any work, thou, nor thy son, nor thy daughter, thy manservant [male slave], nor thy maidservant [female slave], nor thy cattle, nor thy stranger that is within thy gates....	62:9: O you who believe, when the Congregational Prayer is announced on Friday, you shall hasten to the commemoration of God, and drop all business.

Old Testament (Exodus)	Qur'an
20:12: Honour thy father and thy mother: that thy days may be long upon the land which the Lord thy God giveth thee.	17:23-24: You shall be kind to your parents. If one or both of them live to their old age in your lifetime, you shall not say to them any word of contempt nor repel them, and you shall address them in kind words. You shall lower to them the wing of humility and pray: "O Lord! Bestow on them Your blessings just as they cherished me when I was a little child."
20:13: Thou shalt not kill.	17:33: And do not take any human being's life—that God willed to be sacred—other than in [the pursuit of] justice.
20:14: Thou shalt not commit adultery.	17:32: You shall not commit adultery. Surely it is a shameful deed and an evil way.
20:15: Thou shalt not steal. .	60:12: O Prophet! When believing women com to thee to take the oath of fealty to thee, that they will not associate in worship any other thing whatever with God, that they will not commit adultery or fornication, that they will kill their children, that they will not utter slander, intentionally forging falsehood, that they will not disobey thee in any just matter, then do thou receive their fealty, and pray to God to forgive them, for God is Oft-Forgiving, Most Merciful.

Old Testament (Exodus)	Qur'an
20:16: Thou shalt not bear false witness against thy neighbour.	25:72: And (know that the true servants of God are) those who do not bear witness to falsehood.
20:17: Thou shalt not covet thy neighbour's house, thou shalt not covet thy neighbour's wife, nor his manservant [male slave], nor his maidservant [female slave], nor his ox, nor his ass, nor any thing that is thy neighbour's.	4:32: Do not covet the bounties that God has bestowed more abundantly on some of you than on others.

Clearly we have a common heritage coming from Abraham, our great prophet and patriarch. The Qur'an mentions his community and his progeny of prophets. He is a father to all of us.

I was invited to visit, along with other interfaith leaders, the military base of Fort Jackson, an Army training center in North Carolina. They shared with us *The Book of Prayers and Reflections*, which is given to people who join the Army and receive training. I found it very interesting that it lists a number of values. These values are used in the training of our soldiers. For each value in the following list, one can find corresponding Qur'an and Hadith quotations: accountability, community, courage, faith, faithfulness, freedom, generosity, grace, guidance, healing, holiness, honesty, integrity, justice, obedience, peace, prayer, protection, reconciliation, repentance, respect, responsibility, righteousness, service, thankfulness, understanding, wisdom, and worship. As Muslims, is there anything that we disagree with in this list? We fully agree with these values.

In his *The Book of Virtues* (Simon & Schuster: 1993), former secretary of education William Bennett mentions ten virtues that should be taught to our children: self-discipline, compassion, responsibility, friendship, work, courage, perseverance, honesty, loyalty, and faith. Is there anything here with which Muslims disagree? These values are taught in all of our communities. All leaders and religions have very similar points. This becomes very obvious when we examine the golden rule in various traditions:

- Buddhism: "Hurt not others in ways that you yourself would find hurtful." [75]
- Christianity: "All things whatsoever you would that men should do to you, do you even so to them, for this is the law and the prophets." [76]
- Confucianism: "If there is one maxim that ought to be acted upon throughout one's whole life, surely it is the maxim of loving-kindness. Do not unto others what you would not have them do unto you." [77]
- Hinduism: "This is the sum of duty: do nothing unto others what would cause you pain if done unto you." [78]
- Islam: "No one is a believer until he desires for his brother what he desires for himself." [79]
- Judaism: "What is hateful to you, do not unto your fellow man. This is the whole Torah; all the rest is commentary." [80]
- Taoism: "Regard your neighbor's gain as your own gain, and your neighbor's loss as your own loss." [81]
- Zoroastrianism: "That nature alone is good which refrains from doing unto others what it would not do to itself." [82]

This is the common heritage of all people. This one golden rule, if applied seriously, would change the world.

On the human relations level, Western and Islamic civilizations have extraordinary links. We have lived and worked together, and have taken and learned from each other. So, it is not surprising that we have many things in common. We need dialogue so that we can understand these things. But more than anything else, we need to practice the values that we preach, the values about which we talk.

While we have many common values, there are some serious differences. This is why there is a need for dialogue and discussion. I want to mention six values: life, family, sobriety, modesty, freedom, and tolerance. We all agree that human beings have a right to life from conception until death. We believe that it is a sin to kill an innocent person and commit suicide. We believe that abortion is a sin and do not accept euthanasia. We accept capital punishment for certain crimes. So, we must recognize our common values. We cannot say that just because someone does not believe in God he or she does not believe in or care for life.

We need to emphasize that the family is a very important social institution. Of course, Muslims emphasize that sexual relations should only exist among married partners. We emphasize abstinence for those who are single.[83] We believe God has forbidden single-sex marriage and homosexual acts. We also discourage divorce, which affects the family and the extended family.

Muslims believe that all intoxicants are *haram* (forbidden). People have different opinions about intoxicants. Islam takes another position. We do not accept alcoholic drinks and intoxicating drugs. We discourage smoking and all other addictions. This is a very important value, the value of sobriety or keeping the mind clear, because the mind is a gift from God.

Every religion emphasizes modesty. Islam has some specific rules of modesty. For example, Islam says there should be modest dress for men and women and no free mixing between them. Islam is against pornography and any type of immorality in music, films, art, and recreation, for such things do not enhance and build modesty in society.

We firmly believe in the freedom of all people and in the freedom of religion. The Qur'an says there should be no compulsion in religion (*La ikraha fi ad-din*).[84] Religion should be the free choice of all people. We believe in the freedom of expression, with the understanding that no one has the right to falsely abuse and accuse others. So there has to be some understanding. We believe in the freedom of association and the freedom of movement. People should be free to move from one place to another. We believe in the freedom of enterprise, and have detailed laws of permissible and forbidden business practices. We believe in the political freedom of all people of all nations. We believe in pluralism, defined as unity within diversity.

Tolerance is another very important principle for all people. As Muslims, we can say that we do not accept hate, prejudice, or discrimination based on one's color, creed, race, ethnic, linguistic, or national background. We believe that people should be allowed to express their views without disrespecting others. We believe that other people's religion, culture, and heritage should be fully respected. Whether we agree or disagree with someone, we should respect their religion, sacred personalities, sacred scriptures, culture, and heritage.

These important values are shared by our communities. There are areas of agreement and areas of disagreement. But we cannot say that because we disagree with others on various issues that we have nothing in common with them. Even though we have serious differences as regards these six values, we believe that we need to reassert them via education in our schools and in the media. Laws and rules should be made to enforce these values, and those who violate them should be censored and brought to justice. There should be active examples of these morals in society to promote these values, as well as advocacy and support groups, along with continuous dialogue and discussion, in our communities so that we can improve our society.

I want to emphasize that neither Islamophobia nor anti-Americanism will benefit humanity. What is going to help humanity is people sitting together, talking, and exchanging ideas. By doing this, we can discover the many things that we have in common. Let's sit together and discuss our commonalities and respect our differences, for by doing so we can overcome Islamophobia and anti-Americanism.

Do Not Stereotype Evangelicals

Richard Cizik

I
T IS NOT only important for Muslims and Christians to
have dialogue overseas, but also in the United States. In a
manner similar to Muslims, Christian Evangelicals also believe
they are stereotyped. The *Washington Post* once said: "They [Evangelicals]
are poor, uneducated, and easy to command."[85] We are not really poor or
uneducated; but most of all, we are not easy to command. We are an
umbrella organization that includes 45,000 churches, 51 denominations,
and about 30 million people. We are interested in dialoging with
Muslims. We are interested in a better relationship with American
Muslims and with Muslims overseas. We have been described as
"frightening," as "waging a war on America," "loonies," "the American
Taliban," "the first jihadists," and "Ayatollah bin Dobson." Muslims and
evangelicals have something in common: We both stand accused of
things, of producing a theocracy and a jihad.

These stereotypes are not true. We want to engage and love our
neighbors, and most of all Muslims. We want to defend Muslim religious
rights as much as we are interested in defending our own. We believe
that religious liberty is the first and foremost of all religious rights. Our
country was founded on that principle. It is a principle and a right that
we all share. If we as the National Association of Evangelicals (NAE) have
not defended Muslim right in the past, we are open to talking about
how we might defend them better in the future.

There are differences. Fundamentalists constitute 10 percent of the
broad Evangelical umbrella. Although the religious Right is at most 25 to

30 percent of the broad Evangelical movement, its leaders get all the press. As Evangelicals, we are diagnosed rather than heard. It is a kind of psychologizing that makes it possible to dismiss others and their religious beliefs. Good theology will prevent another 9/11, not the Pentagon, intelligence agencies, or the self-satisfied elites who disdain the role of religion in America.

We face parallel challenges. Some of our similarities make things difficult. Our scriptures define us. We believe Evangelicals are the center of moral gravity in America among Protestants. We stand against postmodernism and relativism. We acknowledge our sins of the past. People of all religions need dialogue. Muslims have no interest in minimizing the role of religion in the public sphere in America.

My Muslim friends have told me that Muhammad said: "Happy is the person who finds fault with himself instead of others"[86] and "None of you has faith unless you love for your brother what you love for your self."[87] Evangelicals have to look at themselves, Muslims have to look at themselves, and we have to find some ways to agree, to move forward, and to find common ground. I would suggest that the interfaith dialogue that has occurred over the past 25 years has been deficient, for it has resulted in a lowest common denominator discussion. The result is simply a commitment in the World Council of Religions to say: "Peace and justice." It results in a vacuous call for toleration.

This is not the kind of interfaith dialogue in which Evangelicals are interested. We are interested in a dialogue that acknowledges our differences and our strong commitments. Just as we are scripturally rooted in the Bible, Muslims are scripturally rooted in the Qur'an. Muslims have some difficulties, such as the proliferation of centers of authority and fragmentation, which also exist in our community. We have made statements. The statement we put out in 2003 went around the world. Mainstream Evangelical leaders criticized and called for an end to anti-Islamic rhetoric.[88] It is important for Muslims to acknowledge these steps forward in our community.

I would say that 1,000 years ago, the greatest minds of Christianity, Islam, and Judaism, such as Thomas Aquinas, al-Farabi, and Maimonides, respectively, were all engaged in a fundamental debate about the nature of revelation, faith, reason, law, and political authority. Out of their disagreements, they built a common discourse along and across religious boundaries. This is what is called for at this time in history. A great deal of bridge building needs to be done. That is why I appreciate any opportunity to converse with representatives from groups like CAIR. I hope to help create a kind of positive pluralism—not to be mistaken for relativism—that goes beyond mere tolerance. I can be tolerant of my Muslim neighbors, but that does not build any bridges. It does not help me to get to know him or her. We need to build upon our differences rather than ignore them.

In Virginia, the New Life in Christ Church in Fredericksburg has engaged in dialogue with the Manassas Mosque in Manassas. This is the kind of example I would recommend. Lastly, I would say that we have a high level of religious identification in America. That is probably good. Unfortunately, we have a low level of religious literacy. The program with the Manassas Mosque is an attempt to correct this problem. Changing the stereotypes and prejudices that form fault lines is critical if America is to exercise leadership in the world. It is absolutely essential that these stereotypes and prejudices end. I am committed to ending this type of stereotyping of the Muslim community, and I believe the leadership of the NAE is as well. We call this bridging outward. It is also called bridge building. NAE new documents call for and affirm this approach. So I declare: Let the bridge building begin!

Let's Take Our Shared Values to the Public Square

Shanta Premawardhana

O N MAY 13, 2005, I coordinated a Jewish-Christian dialogue meeting at which a table of representatives from mainstream Jewish organizations and Christian denominations came together. We have been meeting every few months for about a year. This is a tense meeting. It is particularly tense because the past several months one of our member denominations had resolved to study selected faith divestment from businesses and corporations that do business with Israel. So this is a very difficult conversation. Some of our Jewish partners have said they cannot stay in this meeting; other people and I have said that it is at times like this that it is critically important that we talk and not go away from our dialogue.

In thinking about a Christian-Muslim dialogue, I contemplated why we should engage in this encounter? What values are at play? What are the deeply held Biblical values that I bring to the table? I came up with one which I feel is particularly important. It is in the list that Dr. Siddiqi presented.[89] It is the word *reconciliation*. Reconciliation is a very important Biblical affirmation. Christians affirm that they are reconciled to God by virtue of their commitment to Christ. Therefore, we participate in the ministry of reconciliation among each other.

When the members of the early church came together, they felt that bringing people together across social divisions was a very important part of the church's mission. I am not referring to some warm, fuzzy, feel-good kind of thing. Ever since South Africa showed us the way through the Truth and Reconciliation Commission, reconciliation has become a tough-minded, hard-nosed political strategy. Such experiences of reconciliation bring people together across barriers that normally divide, across chasms of fear and raw edges of emotion that exist between people because of the violence that has been perpetrated against them. Reconciliation is a key moral value to me and to the organization that I represent.

The National Council of Churches (NCC), the premier Christian ecumenical organization in the United States, brings together thirty-six Christian denominations, including Protestants of various sorts, Anglicans, and Orthodox. It is a very diverse group of people. Imagine representatives of various Orthodox churches and representatives from the Kerala Church of India sitting together at the same table with representatives from peace-churches like the Quakers, or with representatives from the historic African-American churches like the African Episcopal Church. At this table, you are not allowed to dilute what you believe in or to give up that to which your tradition is committed. In fact, you are asked to be authentic to yourself and to the tradition and faith that you represent. We then come to the table to work out our differences and find our commonalities. It is urgent to bring people together from places that divide us.

This is also true at the interfaith table. I want to bring Jews, Muslims, Hindus, Buddhists, and people of other faiths together with Christians. At that table, we recognize that we are different and that we do not want to dilute our differences. Rather, we must recognize who we are while working to find common ground. Reconciliation is a basic religious value for us.

Right-wing Christian leaders, led by an organization called "Focus on the Family," recently led a simulcast gathering with thousands of people. It was a political rally held in religious garb. They held that Senate Democrats are stalling President Bush's judicial nominees, thereby setting the stage for what has come to be known as the "nuclear option": the right of senators to filibuster. This is one of those tools of checks and balances in our government that our forefathers had the wisdom to institute so that there would not be a tyranny of the majority.

We would say that is fine. They have the right to simulcast and to say whatever they want. There was a problem, however: They claimed that those who voted against their position, were not Christians, or were even anti-Christian. This mentality is working against reconciliation. That kind of thinking is not new. People have been saying that those Christians who do not agree with President Bush and who think differently than the Right on such issues as abortion, gay marriage, and war, are not really Christians. Television talk shows make it seem like Jerry Falwell, Pat Robertson, and Franklin Graham represent Christianity. Thankfully, there is another side to this story.

Just one week after the November 2004 election, the NCC general assembly acknowledged that the national discussion of moral values during the campaign had resulted in a widely held perception of opposing Christian camps in the United States. Our resolution affirmed that Christian values include the work of eliminating poverty, preserving the environment, and promoting peace. One speaker made the point that if the last election was dominated by fear, fundamentalism, and Fox, we are going to be about peace, poverty, and the planet earth.

The NCC is an umbrella organization consisting of about 110,000 churches with about 45 million people. While most of them may not act on these values or think about them at all, a faithful core does. Last year, a poverty mobilization task force campaign called Let Justice Roll went around the country registering poor people to vote. Poor people are often disempowered and rarely participate in the political process. I think we worked to significantly change that dynamic. In 2005, hundreds of people rallied in Washington, DC, stating that the budget is a moral issue—particularly regarding the privatization of Social Security. Social Security checks have kept many people out of poverty. It seems unimaginable that Congress would suggest that Americans should sacrifice that safety net for the uncertainty created by private accounts.

Just recently we ended a boycott of Taco Bell, one of the largest consumers of tomatoes grown in Florida. In Florida, there are mostly migrant workers who are treated like slave laborers. When churches wanted to negotiate with Taco Bell about the plight of their tomato workers, Taco Bell did not want to come to the table. After about three years, Taco Bell came to the table and the boycott was lifted.

We are currently working on the issue of health care and trying to provide health care coverage for the 45 million uninsured people. We engage churches in many campaigns such as these. Right now we are working on a new project, Making Poverty History, based on the work of Professor Jeffrey Sachs at Columbia University. We are discussing how to mobilize our churches around that.

I should also point out what we have done about the war in Iraq, from organizing people in different localities (e.g., street corners and churches) to holding candle-light vigils against the impending war. Religious communities were the core of the grassroots movement against that war, as well as trade unions and student and women's organizations. We are at the forefront of that, and also on issues related to the environment. Right now, 1,400 religious leaders have signed a document called "God's

Mandate for Care for the Earth." For many Christians, Biblical values are not just abortion and gay marriage. There is a significant difference between the values espoused by conservative Christians and mainstream Christians.

I visited Sri Lanka and Indonesia after the tsunami. I went to churches in those countries to say that we want to stand in solidarity with them during this time. And I brought a message back to American churches to say that at this point in time, we need to listen to and learn from Asia's pain. Their leaders pointed at one basic value each time. They said that building community is the most important priority. That is related to the value of reconciliation with which I began. The tsunami destroyed families, extended families, and communities. When non-governmental organizations and other communities came in from the outside, they had specific agendas that did not meet the exact needs of the local communities. They brought their agendas to the table, a reality that created further disruption in these communities.

In Indonesia, there was a big issue with a Christian group from Virginia attempting to adopt 300 Indonesian Muslim children so that they might be raised as Christians. These are the types of things that are against reconciliation and building community. Asian church leaders said that if there is one thing to say to the folks in the United States, it is to build communities rather than break down communities.

One final thing: The building of communities has direct implications on Muslim-Christian relations. This February, when our interfaith commission met in St. Petersburg, Florida, we had a session with representatives from CAIR in Tampa. They told this group about the kinds of issues they have so eagerly been working on, issues that Muslims have to face, such as U.S. Patriot Act. We brought a resolution to our governing body that stated that we stand with Muslims at such a time as this, when our Muslim brothers and sisters are struggling under the burden of the U.S. Patriot Act. We stand in solidarity with Muslims. That is how building coalitions works. That is how reconciliation works. We can work together to take away some of the draconian measures in the U.S. Patriot Act and stand together against them. When moral values are politicized, we need to affirm the moral values on which we are working. Together, we will make that happen.

THE ROLE OF AMERICAN MUSLIMS

LET US BE ON THE SIDE OF AMERICA'S GREATNESS

Cherrif Bassiouni

AFTER 9/11, MANY so-called Muslim leaders were going around the country apologizing for Islam. The events of 9/11 are a crime, but that does not mean that Islam as a religion is responsible or that Muslims need to apologize for Islam. People were eager to point out that Islam is the same as Judaism and Christianity. I disagree with this approach and would not apologize for Islam. All Muslims should be proud of being Muslim. Why do we need to be ashamed of being Muslim? Why can Jews be proud of being Jewish and wear a yarmulke, or Christians be proud of being Christian and go to church, but Muslims must be ashamed of Islam? Let me remind people that we are in the United States because we believe in the constitution and in basic freedoms, including freedom of religion. As Muslims in America, we should not give up this right no matter how difficult some people want to make it for us.

When 9/11 happened, I saw a mirror of America with two images. The America I believe in, the America with people of courage, including the firemen who risked their lives to save others in the burning buildings, the people who survived the terrible event, and their families who endured the pain of that event, and continued to act as decent human beings. I also saw an image of an intolerant America, an America that was willing to abandon the constitution and civil rights. I saw people who were willing to profit from the crisis in which the country found itself. I saw an image of those who wanted to profit from their ideology, to wage war abroad and violate people's rights at home. This was the ugly side of America.

But in the history of this country, there has always been the side of greatness fighting with a certain side of ugliness. One hundred or 140 years in the history of any nation is very little time, but this many years ago Americans were still fighting over slavery. Even though the Civil War ended in 1865, it took until the 1960s to enact civil rights legislation giving African Americans equal rights and protection from segregation.

Even today, we live in a fundamentally racist society of whites, blacks, and people of color. It is not easy to forge a nation, especially a nation that is represented by people from all over the world. America is an extraordinary experiment that has never happened anywhere else in the world. But this experiment is still a work in progress. It will only succeed if those who periodically find themselves at the bottom of the poltical food chain are willing to fight. It will succeed when those who bear the brunt of discrimination, persecution, and religious intolerance are willing to stand firmly for their rights. If, in the 1960s, we did not have a civil rights movement in which African Americans were willing to take to the streets and fight both under the banner of Martin Luther King, Jr. (the peaceful banner) and under the more violent banner that we saw in 1967 and 1968, African Americans would still be sitting on different sides of the room, drinking from different fountains, and riding in the back of the bus.

There is not a single historical experience in any society in the world in which the oppressed have been given their rights on a silver platter. There is only one way people can gain their rights: They have to fight for them. Muslims now have to ask themselves a question: "Do we want to be the new Uncle Toms of America?" The African Americans have given up that role. The Muslims are now the new Uncle Toms.

Muslims are eager to apologize for Islam. Yet Muslim societies, because if we are, there is a great deal about which to talk. Muslims and Muslim societies are deficient in so many ways. Muslim leaders in Muslim countries are, for the most part, corrupt and cruel people. There is no democracy. I do not suggest that American Muslims remain silent in the face of these things. I am not arguing that we should be quiet regarding the horrible actions of Osama bin Laden, al-Zarqawi, or others. On the contrary, I would encourage everyone to condemn these characters because their crimes violate Islam and are directed against all of us. But there is a difference between having to condemn an Osama bin Laden or an al-Zarqawi, which I do, and my having to defend the Prophet because Pat Robertson or Jerry Falwell wants to call him a terrorist. I wonder what the response would be if a group of Muslims headed by one of their leaders said that Jesus Christ or Moses was a terrorist. What would happen to someone who said that?

The point is American Muslims are at the bottom of the ladder. As we have seen throughout American history, there is always a social group at the bottom of the ladder. So at one time it was the Irish, and the Irish made it up. And then it was the Italians, and the Italians made it up. For 200 years it was the African Americans, and they finally broke away and made it up. Although I am not too sure that they have made it too far up, at least they are well on their way. And now it is our turn. I suggest that we look at the history of other groups that have been targeted.

I am not necessarily sure that this current form of targeting has particular political purposes. I am sure there is some of that. But I think this is cyclical in American society. American society always needs to have a villain. There has to be someone who is a villain, who looks bad. Among our people, we lend ourselves to it. A lot of our people look strange and act strange. I remember the 1970s caricatures of the Saudi *shaykhs* (tribal leaders) because of the rising oil prices. Even though the price went up because of the American oil companies, it was the shaykhs who were portrayed in a negative way. So it is alright. We can accept a little of this and they can make fun of us. We can make fun of them as well. We do not have to take it too seriously.

But there are things for which we have to stand up and be counted, and for which we have to fight. There is absolutely no reason for the American Muslim community to accept the types of insults and blasphemous remarks made by people like Pat Robertson and Jerry Falwell, or the things that Daniel Pipes and others write on certain websites. This is   totally intolerable. One might say that this is un-American and that this is a free country. If these people are free to say what they say, then we should be free to fight back. We have no reason for sitting back while these remarks are being made. If we do, then we deserve everything that falls back upon us.

There is a little bit of bad news and a little bit of good news. The good news is that those who are bigots, intolerant, and anti-Muslim are very few in this country. That is the good news. Frankly, we should not waste our time dealing with them. We should spend our time constructively reaching out to the majority of Americans, who are decent, open-minded, tolerant, people who would welcome us with open arms if we reached out to them and informed them of our positions. We have to do this with a great deal of courage and openness. We have to be able to accept blame whenever its assignation is justified.

Also, we have to have the courage to speak out against those things that are happening in Muslim societies, in the name of Islam, that we know in our hearts to be wrong. We must have the courage to say such things are wrong. In that respect, we will do nothing more than what the Prophet (peace be upon him) admonished us to do. If you see a wrong, you must correct it with your hand if you can; and if you cannot, then with your tongue; and if you cannot, then at least know that it is wrong in your heart. According to the Prophet (peace be upon him), that is the weakest form of faith. So why should we be among those who have the weakest faith? Why should our faith not be stronger?

When we see a wrong, we should act to correct it. If we can do so by our hands, we should. If we cannot correct a wrong with our hands, then we should try to correct it with our tongues and other means. Ultimately, if we cannot, because we are unable to do so, then at least we should never accept a wrong in our hearts when it is committed, either against us or against others, because part of our belief in Islam is not to have double standards. If we are going to fight people who have double standards and who apply double standards to us, then we must make sure that we do not have double standards.

The task ahead of us is quite large. First of all, we need to believe in ourselves, our faith, the constitution, and our basic human rights if we are to stand up and fight for them. When we do that, we have to do it intelligently. We have to learn how to organize, divide tasks, and make sure that different people do different things based upon their expertise and specialty. Above all, we have to give up the constant struggle of every one of us to be a caliph or a leader. We have to learn to be soldiers before we are generals. We have to learn that the first thing a soldier does is a little bit of work. We cannot all sit on top of a white horse, point our finger somewhere, and wait for somebody else to do the work.

These are very simple realities, and these are the realities we all have adjusted to in this country by earning a degree, entering a profession, participating in society, and living by the very rules that have made this society so strong. So why is it that when it comes to our community affairs, so many of us forget about our responsibilities? On Monday morning we are perfectly capable of disciplining ourselves. We drive and steer our car in the middle of the lane. We get to work on time and produce accordingly. And then what happens on Friday? We forget our discipline and responsibilities when we get together. I think it is time that we keep these lessons in mind at all times and start working on the basics.

In conclusion, the feeling I want to share is my sense of pride, but not in the wrong sense of the word. By pride I mean that I am proud of being a human being created by Allah (God) and being the kind of creature that the Qur'an speaks of as having been the object of *takrim* (honor) from Allah. Of all of the creatures that Allah has created, He conferred the highest dignity on human beings. And so, as a creature of Allah upon whom this dignity has been bestowed, I would like to see Muslims as well as all human beings realize that we are part of the same humanity that Allah created. As He says in the Qur'an: "Allah has created you, men and women, peoples, and tribes, so that you may inhabit the world."[90] Allah has created humanity, consisting of men and women, peoples, and tribes, to inhabit this universe. So we are a part of humanity as a whole. We believe that there is only one God, Who has created us. We believe in His infinite wisdom. Allah has communicated to us a message that we call *religion*, which has come through a succession of revelations given to Abraham, Moses, Jesus, and Muhammad.

And so, being part of this humanity created by Allah, I have a sense of pride in being a human being, in being a Muslim, and in having devoted my life to humanity and human rights. And frankly, I do not feel like I have to, nor do I want to, explain or justify that to anyone. I think that in every one of us there is a reflection of Adam. So this is what I want to tell American Muslims at this juncture of our history: Allah gave you that dignity, and it is enough for each and every one of us and every person to feel a certain sense of pride. Only if you feel this dignity will you be able to stand up and fight for your rights, refuse to accept oppression, stand up for what is right, and commit yourself to do the work necessary to accomplish a good result. It all starts with whether or not you believe in your inherent dignity as human beings and as Muslims. If you do, then we will succeed. If you do not, then we will not.

American Muslims Are Playing a Role in Bridging the Chasm

Asma Afsaruddin

WHAT CAN AMERICAN Muslims do about anti-American sentiment in the Muslim world? What can the American government do about anti-Americanism? To answer these questions, it is important to think about what Americans in general—Muslims and non-Muslims—can do in tandem to address this problem, because, obviously, neither group operates or can operate in a vacuum.

First, the role of American Muslims in this endeavor: Admittedly, American Muslims can play a special role in combating anti-American sentiment. Precious opportunities come their way when they travel to Islamic societies and, better still, if they are able to reside there for a period of time. Let me draw on my personal experience. In the spring of 2004, I lived in Cairo for about four months during my sabbatical year. I was accompanied by my husband, who, however, lived for the most part in another town, Luxor, in the south, that is considerably smaller and far less cosmopolitan than Cairo. This was our first time back in an Arab Muslim country after 9/11 and after the American invasion of Iraq.

When people became aware of the fact that we were Americans, it made no appreciable difference in their attitudes and behavior toward us, as far as we could tell. This was true of shopkeepers, of people whom we stopped on the street to ask for directions, or of academics with whom we had contact, or of friends we had known in the past. Separately, our experiences still remained the same. In bustling, sophisticated Cairo, as an American Muslim of non-European ancestry who speaks Arabic, I blended in easily and encountered no hostility whatsoever.

To the contrary, I was sometimes the target of questions born out of concern and pity. Had I suffered from unfair profiling and discrimination on account of my being Muslim in post-9/11 America, some of them would ask? Was I constantly under a cloud of suspicion for being Muslim? Was I constantly being asked to explain myself, to defend my religion and practices to hostile, uncomprehending people? There was a lot of compassion expressed toward American Muslims, who, they had heard, were being unfairly treated and being scape-goated for the crimes of a minority. I had heard similar questions on an earlier trip to Turkey. The irony of this should be noted: America has long served as the refuge for minority groups fleeing from perse-cution and harassment overseas. That American Muslims now may be considered overseas as victims of persecution and deserving of pity is a sad, trenchant commentary on the state of civil liberties within the United States as they apply to us.

My husband, who is Euro-American and speaks a modest amount of Arabic, never encountered any anti-American hostility in Luxor or Cairo. This was during the height of the American occupation of Iraq and as the tale of atrocities committed at Abu Ghraib unfolded. Instead, he met the proverbial unfailing Arab hospitality, being invited to simple homes sometimes in spite of his being American, or maybe I should say because he is American, and only suffering on occasion from the persistent demands of street vendors and the occasional greedy cab driver, something that I was subjected to as well (and with which many tourists are familiar). Were we in some kind of a dream world?

I have a feeling that things would have been different if my husband and I had breezed into Cairo, dragged down by television cameras, thrust a mike into someone's face, and asked a pointed question like: "What do you think of the US government and its policies in the Middle East?" I have a feeling we would have gotten an earful. During my stay in Cairo, I did not go out of my way to talk politics with relative strangers. I once initiated a political conversation with my landlord, who is from a prominent Cairene upper-class family, and he was decidedly uncomfortable. He remarked he and his wife, both physicians, preferred to concern themselves with their professions and their children's educations, both of which kept them quite occupied. And this, in fact, is the overwhelming reality for most people in Egypt, and I suspect, in most parts of the Islamic world, except for Iraq, Afghanistan, and the Palestinian territories, where America's military might is in your face literally or by proxy, and your daily life is shaped by this basic fact. For most everyone else, America remains an abstraction and a country of paradoxes.

There is America the genuinely beautiful, which includes a significant cross-section of its people whose hearts bleed for the less fortunate, who are critical of the rapacious underbelly of globalization, who support their government when it stands up for American ideals, and who criticize their government when it compromises them at home and abroad. It is a truism to say that most people abroad often distinguish between the American people and their government, that they are savvy enough not to conflate the two, and that a significant number of them admire many aspects of American society but at the same time criticize certain foreign policy measures adopted by the government.

I have found this verified by many American friends and

colleagues who have visited parts of the Islamic world recently, particularly the Middle East. The *Christian Science Monitor* recently ran an article about a lawyer from Washington, DC, who now lives in Damascus, Syria, in order to learn Arabic. It quoted this man as saying: "Being here, that is in Syria, has been incredibly enlightening. All the Arabs I've met have this amazing ability to distinguish between Americans and the American government. I wish I had a nickel for every time I've been told: 'I hate your government, welcome to my country!'" "It gives me hope," he continued, "for the future of East-West relations."[91]

And so I find it useful to remind some of my friends and interlocutors, both in the States and in the Arab world, of this basic distinction and how it has become more meaningful than ever. I also find it necessary to inform my Muslim friends abroad that better educated Americans do not react in a visceral way toward Muslims and Arabs and South Asians, and that their greater access to more reliable information has made for more nuanced and sophisticated views on their part. It is usually the not-so-well-educated and ill-informed segments of American society who are particularly susceptible to powerful media sound bytes that propagate certain stereotypes of Muslims and repeatedly convey images of a violent Middle East. This situation is mirrored in the Middle East: Better educated Arabs had far more nuanced and polychromatic views of America and Americans than did their less educated compatriots, and they tended to be more aware of the internal diversity of opinions within pluralistic America.

A survey conducted by the Pew Research Center for the People and the Press and the Pew Forum on Religion and Public Life in 2004 confirms certain trends. According to this survey, nearly half of all

Americans believe that the United States government should restrict the civil liberties of American Muslims. The survey also found that Republicans and people who describe themselves as highly religious are more apt to support curtailing Muslims' civil liberties than Democrats or people who are less religious. Researchers also found that respondents who pay more attention to television news are more likely to fear terrorist attacks and support limiting the rights of American Muslims.

Interestingly, these results tallied very nicely with the survey conducted more recently by Cornell University that found, for example, that 44 percent favor at least some restrictions on the civil liberties of American Muslims. This survey showed that 27 percent of respondents support requiring all American Muslims to register where they live with the federal government, 22 percent favor racial profiling to identify potential terrorist threats, and 29 percent think that undercover agents should infiltrate Muslim civic and volunteer organizations to keep tabs on their activities and fundraising.

This kind of bad news finds corroboration in the study recently conducted by CAIR and picked up by the Associated Press, which documents a "disturbing rise in anti-Muslim hate crimes and in the total number of civil rights cases." The report showed a 49 percent increase in civil rights violations in 2004 over 2003 and a 52 percent rise in incidents of confirmed or suspected bias crimes committed against Muslims. So there is a lot of bad news, and these statistics are cause for grave alarm.

On the other hand, if one scrutinizes these surveys carefully, there is cause for cautious optimism. One can even derive important policy implications from it. A solid majority of liberal Democrats (56 percent) say they have a favorable opinion of Islam, while a plurality of secular and Catholic Americans (50 percent and 43 percent, respectively) have a positive impression of Islam, as compared with evangelical Protestants and conservative Republicans. On balance, the Pew report noted, younger Americans, those under age 30, hold a more favorable view of Islam. Forty-eight percent say civil liberties should not be restricted in any way. These important micro-differences point, above all, to the difference that education might make in the political and cultural views of individuals and whole groups.

Unfortunately, the Cornell survey did not refer to the respondents' education levels, a serious shortcoming. But one may assume that liberals, in general, tend to be better educated, more sophisticated in their worldviews, and more receptive to difference and diversity. Secular and younger people also share this profile. The Catholic response may be explained by the fact that post-Vatican II Catholic church teachings are certainly more ecumenical and inclusive than evangelical Protestant beliefs. Clearly, education and the inculcation of tolerance must remain a top priority. Our work is cut out for us if we are going to combat negative stereotypes of Muslims effectively.

After 9/11, after the American invasion of Iraq, and after Abu Ghraib, there remain Muslims in the Islamic heartlands who still admire that for which America is meant to stand: precious political and economic freedoms as well as an unqualified regard for everyone's human dignity and rights. But the Patriot Act and the curtailment of civil liberties for a significant number of American Muslims, not to mention the harassment of many non-American Muslims, have dimmed America's luster. There is no doubt about this. It has given rise to disenchantment with specific American government policies both at home and abroad, which is wrongly equated with a blanket form of anti-Americanism. Within our own borders, one remembers how many Americans (mostly better educated) expressed the wish to emigrate after the last elections. The demarcation of Blue states from the Red states drove home the country's polarization along cultural lines and along the fault lines of contested ethical and moral values. The moral disillusionment is very real.

What can the current American government do about it? It should take a long, hard look at the unfortunate reversal of civil liberties that has taken place in this country and that has tarnished America's good name. This country has genuine security concerns and is entitled to take effective security measures, but without compromising anyone's basic rights and liberties as citizens and as human beings, whether in this country or abroad. The rule of law remains our best defense against fear and insecurity.

There has to be an acknowledgment on the part of our government officials that specific American foreign policy measures, particularly in regard to the Israeli-Palestinian conflict, remain the biggest stumbling block to winning hearts abroad. An initiative funded several years ago by the Pew Charitable Trusts called Project Maps (Muslim Americans in the Public Square) documented the state of the Muslim community in America. The first systematic polling of American Muslims showed that most agree with the actions taken by the United States in Afghanistan against al-Qaidah and the Taliban. However, a majority also felt that American policy in the Middle East contributes to hostility overseas against the United States.

Finally, the American government has to be consistent in its support of democracy and criticism of tyranny worldwide, and not only when it is expedient. It should not play—or appear to play—favorites and should hold everyone up to the same standards of human rights and conformity to democratic standards of governance. When American citizens, Muslims and non-Muslims, demand that our government behave at all times in accordance with the highest ideals enshrined in our constitution, we should not have to face the charge emanating from certain quarters of fomenting anti-Americanism and having our loyalty called into question. It is precisely because we are loyal and concerned citizens that we must continue to insist that certain core principles of decency and fair and equal treatment for all under the law be upheld at all times and for all peoples by those who govern us. As Dale Carnegie might have put it, it is the only way to win friends and influence people.

NOTES

NOTES

[1] Such findings are supported by public opinion polls commissioned by CAIR in 2004 and 2005. See CAIR, *American Public Opinion about Islam and Muslims* (Washington, DC, 2005).

[2] http://pewresearch.org/pubs/6/arab-and-muslim-perceptions-of-the-united-states.

[3] http://pewglobal.org/reports/display.php?PageID=831.

[4] David Cole, "The New McCarthyism: Repeating History in the War on Terrorism," in *Harvard Civil Rights-Civil Liberties Law Review* Vol. 38, No. 1, 2003, p.1-30.

[5] http://www.cair-net.org/includes/Anti-TerrorList.pdf.

[6] Michael Scheuer, former CIA Head of Bin Laden Unit, concurs with this assessment in his book *Imperial Hubris* (Washington, DC: Brassey's Inc., 2004).

[7] PIPA, *Muslim Public Opinion on US Policy, Attacks on Civilians and al Qaeda*, (Washington, DC, 2007). The poll was conducted in April. See at: http://www.worldpublicopinion.org/pipa/pdf/apr07/START_Apr07_rpt.pdf.

[8] Jennifer Harper, "Curtain raised on documentary PBS shelved," *Washington Times*, April 25, 2007.

[9] Frank Gaffney, "A Film PBS Want Unaired," *Washington Times*, April 13, 2007.

[10] See full Islamophobia report by Runnymede Trust, *Islamophobia: A Challenge for Us All*. (London, UK, 1997).

[11] See an extensive account of Muslim slaves in Sylviane A. Diouf *Servants of Allah: African Muslims Enslaved in the Americas* (New York: NY, New York University Press, 1998).

[12] CAIR, *American Muslim Voters: A Demographic Profile* (Washington, DC, October 24, 2006).

[13] *Ibid.*

[14] http://pewforum.org/publications/surveys/islam.pdf.

[15] http://abcnews.go.com/sections/us/World/sept11_islampoll_030911.html.

[16] http://www.cair-net.org/downloads/pollresults.ppt.

[17] http://www.news.cornell.edu/releases/Dec04/Muslim.Poll.bpf.html.

[18] CAIR, *The Status of Muslim Civil Rights in the United States*, 2007.

Notes

[19] Frederick C. Luebke, *Bonds of Loyalty: German-Americans and World War I* (DeKalb: Northern Illinois University Press, 1974), p. xiii.

[20] Paul W. Glad, *The History of Wisconsin, Volume V: War, a New Era, and Depression, 1914-1940* (Madison, State Historical Society of Wisconsin, 1990), p. 16.

[21] Quoted in an article by another notable accuser of Protestant clergy, Gerald L. K. Smith, "Communism in the Churches," *The Cross and the Flag* 14, No. 10 (January 1956), p.9.

[22] For the debates and issues in the Methodist Church as seen at the time, see Ralph Lord Roy, *Apostles of Discord* (Boston: MA, The Beacon Press, 1953), chapter 13.

[23] Samuel P. Huntington, "The Hispanic Challenge," *Foreign Policy* (March/ April, 2004), p. 31. His analysis is presented more fully in Samuel P. Huntington, *Who are we? The challenges to America's national identity* (New York, NY: Simon & Schuster, 2004).

[24] Huntington, "The Hispanic Challenge," p. 31.

[25] See, for example, the description of Germans in Montana in Jim Robbins, "Silence Broken, Pardons Granted 88 Years After Crimes of Sedition," *New York Times*, May 3, 2006, pp.1, 19.

[26] Here I am borrowing Richard Bulliet's use of the concept of the civilizational *master narrative* in his *The Case for Islamo-Christian Civilization* (New York, NY: Coumbia University Press: 2004). I prefix the adjective *supremacist* to emphasize the degree to which these grand cultural identity myths exalt the home civilization at the cost of denigrating the civilization of the other.

[27] Learn more about Ms. O'Halloran and her important work in fostering cross-cultural and interreligious understanding by visiting her website: www.susanohalloran.com.

[28] Scott Alexander, "Inalienable Rights?: Muslims in the U.S. since September 11th," *Journal of Islamic Law and Culture*, Vol 7, No. 1 (spring/summer, 2002).

[29] Every subjugated people harbors a social Darwinist suspicion, albeit usually short-lived, that the culture of the dominant other must be superior to that of the indige-nous self. Otherwise, how could the former have come to be in the dominant position in the first place?

[30] *Qur'an* 49:13.

[31] *Qur'an* 5:8.

Notes

[32] Remarks by Eleanor Roosevelt at the presentation of "*In Your Hands: A Guide for Community Action for the Tenth Anniversary of the Universal Declaration of Human Rights.*" to the U.N. Commission on Human Rights on March 27, 1958. Cited from: http://www.udhr.org/history/inyour.htm.

[33] www.history.ucsb.edu/faculty/marcuse/niem.htm.

[34] http://www.newamericancentury.org/RebuildingAmericasDefenses.pdf.

[35] www.israeleconomy.org/strat1.htm.

[36] The Pew Research Center for the People and the Press is a respected independent and nonpartisan research organization that "provides information on the issues, attitudes and trends shaping America and the world." See http://people-press.org.

[37] "Plurality Sees Islam as More Likely to Encourage Violence," The Pew Research Center for the People & The Press, September 9, 2004.

[38] Suzanne Goldenberg, "Islamophobia worse in America now than after 9/11, survey finds," *Guardian* (March 10, 2006). A CBS News poll produced the following findings: Unfavorable attitudes toward Islam had increased from 33 percent in February 2002 to 36 percent in February 2006, while favorable attitudes toward the religion had decreased from 30 percent in February 2002 to 23 percent in February 2006. See the CBS News Poll of 27 February 27 2006 ("President Bush, The Ports, and Iraq," February 22-26, 2006). The poll also showed that 56 percent of respondents said that the violent Muslim reaction to the Danish cartoon controversy was not justified, compared with only 9 percent of respondents who said the reaction was justified.

[39] "Plurality Sees Islam as More Likely to Encourage Violence," The Pew Research Center for the People & The Press (September 9, 2004) and "Fewer Say Islam Encourages Violence," The Pew Research Center for the People & The Press (July 26, 2005).

[40] According to the CBS News Poll, this figure was up from 35 percent in March 2002. See the CBS News Poll of February 26, 2006.

[41] Goldenberg, *Ibid.*

[42] ABC News/*Washington Post* Poll: "Views of Islam – 3/5/06."

[43] Chicago Council on Foreign Relations, *Worldviews 2002: American Public Opinion and Foreign Policy*, p. 49. The report goes on to say that "By large, 39 point

gaps, the public is more favorable to decreasing legal immigration (57 percent vs. 18 percent) and to combating international terrorism by restricting immigration from Arab and Muslim countries (79 percent vs. 40 percent)," p.72.

44 Susan Page, "On Security, public draws blurred lines," USA Today (August 3, 2005). The USA Today/Gallup Poll, conducted in the period of July 22-24, 2005, with a sample of more than 1,000 respondents.

45 As we will see below, this is part of the problem. When news program do deal with Islam, Muslims, and Arabs, they do so, more often than not, in the context of bad news: the Iraq war, terrorism, suicide bombings, the Palestinian-Israeli conflict, Osama bin laden and al-Qaidah, and so on.

46 "Fewer Say Islam Encourages Violence," The Pew Research Center for the People & The Press (July 26, 2005).

47 Pew Poll, "Views of Muslim-Americans Hold Steady after London Bombings," (July 26, 2005).

48 For the complete ABC News/Washington Post Poll, "Views of Islam – 3/5/06." See http://abcnews.go.com/images/International/Islam_views.pdf.

49 Pew Poll, "Views of Muslim-Americans Hold Steady," pp.6-7.

50 In other words, the poll established a relationship between one's greater degree of conservatism and the likelihood that he or she is likely to have negative or unfavorable views of Islam.

51 Pew Poll, "Views of Islam Remain Sharply Divided" (September 9, 2004). The Pew Poll states: "On balance, younger Americans, those under age 30, hold a more favorable view of Islam." We can speculate about the reasons for this: younger Americans are more likely to be open-minded then their older compatriots in addition to being more likely to know or interact regularly with Muslim Americans.

52 Stated differently, in their daily lives, where do Americans hear about and where are they exposed to information about Islam, Muslims, and Arabs?

53 This has significance for Muslims, Arabs, and Islam, but possibly only as part of a more general phenomenon.

54 "Alias" and "Threat Matrix" are on ABC, "The Agency" was on CBS for two seasons, "24" shows on Fox, "The Grid" is on TNT, and "Sleeper Cell" is on Showtime. "DHS" (Department of Homeland Security) was produced by Steeple

Notes

Productions, and an article about the show claimed that both President Bush and the former Department of Homeland Security head had endorsed the program! See Jeffrey Jolson-Colburn, "Bush Backs New Television TV Series" at: w.eonline.com/News/Items/0,1,13584,00.html?tnews.

[55] See the show's self-description at www.tv.com/sleeper-cell/show/28827/summary.html.

[56] In fact, what might also be different or new are the "good Arabs" or "good Muslims" that occasionally appear in these programs. Having a few Arabs and Muslims who are *not* terrorists, however, quickly becomes a way to depict other Arabs and Muslims as terrorists and religious fanatics while claiming not to reproduce negative stereotypes and bigotry. It becomes an excuse to claim that not all Arabs and Muslims are portrayed negatively in any given program.

[57] Possibly, and most notably, former Italian Prime Minister Silvio Berlusconi has spoken of the superiority of the West and Christianity.

[58] Falwell's comments led to riots in the Indian city of Solapur. Muslim youths protesting his remarks clashed with Hindus and police, leaving eight people dead and ninety injured. See the *Washington Post* (October 15, 2002).

[59] Pat Robertson is a popular televangelist on the Christian Broadcasting Network and the host of the "700 Club" program. See "US Leaders Asked to Repudiate Televangelist's Anti-Islam Remarks," www.cair.com/default.asp?Page=articleView&id=2052&theType=NR and www.pbs.org/wnet/religionandethics/week616/cover.html. Franklin Graham also said: "The God of Islam is not the same God of the Christian or the Judeo-Christian faith. It is a different God, and I believe a very evil and a very wicked religion."

[60] Boykin has since claimed that when speaking of an "idol" he was not referring to Islam, but to corruption, wealth, and similar things. However, this is difficult to believe in the context of his other statements. "American Muslim Organizations call for removal of General Boykin," www.archives2005.ghazali.net/html/gen_boykin.html. Also see the CBS News interview with Boykin at: www.cbsnews.com/stories/2004/09/15/60II/main643650.shtml.

149

[61] The number of anti-Islamic books and Web sites has increased significantly over the last few years. Refer to Khaled Abou El Fadl's lecture at the American University in Cairo (March 13, 2006).

[62] Pipes' article appeared in *Front Page Magazine* (March 14, 2006). See "Sudden Jihad Syndrome," at: www.frontpagemag.com/Articles/ReadArticle.asp?ID=21630.

[63] Bernard Lewis, *What Went Wrong: The Clash between Islam and Modernity in the Middle East* (New York, NY: Harper Perennial, 2003).

[64] For just one relatively recent example of Friedman's ideas, see his article on the London bombings: "If it's a Muslim Problem, It Needs a Muslim Solution," *New York Times* (July 8, 2005): "When jihadist-style bombings happen in Riyadh, that is a Muslim-Muslim problem. ... But when [al-Qaidah]-like bombings come to the London Underground, *that becomes a civilizational problem*. Every Muslim living in a Western society suddenly becomes a suspect, becomes a potential walking bomb. And when that happens, it means Western countries are going to be tempted to crack down even harder on their own Muslim populations." (emphasis added) See www.nytimes.com/2005/07/08/opinion/08friedman.html?ex=1278475200&en=a1 cbffb46f2ac7d0&ei=5088.

[65] See the Human Rights Watch Report, "We are Not the Enemy: Hate Crimes Against Arabs, Muslims and those perceived to be Arab or Muslim After September 11" (November 2002). The report states: "While comprehensive and reliable national statistics are not available, Arab and Muslim groups report more than two thousand September 11-related backlash incidents. The Federal Bureau of Investigation reported a seventeen-fold increase in anti-Muslim crimes nationwide during 2001. In Los Angeles County and Chicago, officials reported fifteen times the number of anti-Arab and anti-Muslim crimes in 2001 compared to the preceding year." Available at www.hrw.org/reports/2002/usahate/.

[66] On July 28, 2005, a group of American Muslim scholars, meeting under the umbrella of the Fiqh Council of North America, issued the following fatwa: "Islam strictly condemns religious extremism and the use of violence against innocent lives. There is no justification in Islam for extremism or terrorism. Targeting civilians' life and property through suicide bombings or any other method of attack is *haram* (forbidden) and those who commit these barbaric acts are criminals, not martyrs ...

Notes

In the light of the teachings of the Qur'an and Sunnah we clearly and strongly state: 1. All acts of terrorism targeting civilians are *haram* (forbidden) in Islam. 2. It is *haram* for a Muslim to cooperate with any individual or group that is involved in any act of terrorism or violence. 3. It is the civic and religious duty of Muslims to cooperate with law enforcement authorities to protect the lives of all civilians. We issue this fatwa following the guidance of our scripture, the Qur'an, and the teachings of our Prophet Muhammad—peace be upon him." Cited at www.cair-net.org/default.asp?Page=articleView&id=1675&theType=NR. See also www.washingtonpost.com/wp-dyn/content/article/2005/07/27/AR2005072702082.html.

[67] *Qur'an*, 16:120.

[68] *Qur'an*, 3:110.

[69] *Qur'an*, 49:13.

[70] Karen Armstrong, *The Battle For God* (New York, NY: Ballantine Books, 2001).

[71] Schweiker, William, "Religious Conviction and the Intellectual's Responsibility" in *Criterion* , Autumn 2003, pp.10-19.

[72] Martin Luther King Jr., *Strength to Love* (Philadelphia, PA: Fortress Press, 1981), p.4.

[73] Malcolm X,, *The Autobiography of Malcolm X*, (New York, NY: Ballantine Books, 1965), p.366.

[74] *Qur'an*, 4:1.

[75] *Udana Varga*, 5:18.

[76] *Matthew*, 7:12.

[77] *Analects*, 15:23.

[78] *Mahabharata*, 5:1517

[79] *Musnad Ahmdd bin Hanbal,* Hadith No. 8034 and 16220.

[80] *Talmud*, Shabbat 31a; *Tobit* 4:15.

[81] *T'ai Shang Kan-Ying P'ien*, 213-218.

[82] *Dadistan-i Dinik*, 94:5.

[83] See "Book of Fasting," in *Sahih al-Bukhari*, Hadith No. 1806; and "Book of Marriage," in *Sahih Muslim*, Hadith No. 1400.

[84] *Qur'an* 2:256.

[85] The *Washington Post*, February 1, 1993. Cited from: http://www.nationalcenter.org/2005/07/poor-uneducated-and-easy-to-command.html.

Notes

[86] http://www.unification.net/ws/theme143.htm#05.

[87] Hadith 13 of *Forty Hadith by An-Nawawi*. Cited from http://www.aflcio.org/join-aunion/faith/upload/page33.pdf.

[88] See, for example, criticism of Ted Haggard, President of NAE at
http://www.plastic.com/comments.html;sid=03/05/09/11495808;cid=121.
Also, see transcript of a PBS interview with Diane Knippers, President of Institute on Religion and Democracy on March 9, 2003. Cited from:
http://www.pbs.org/wnet/religionandethics/transcripts/636.html.

[89] See p.110.

[90] *Qur'an*, 49:13.

[91] *Christian Science Monitor*, May 10, 2005.